Guild Press of Indiana, Inc.

Indianapolis, Indiana

TUCKER TALKS

FRED C. TUCKER, Jr.

Guild Press of Indiana
6000 Sunset Lane
Indianapolis, IN 46208

Guild Press of Indiana, Inc.
6000 Sunset Lane
Indianapolis, IN 46208

Printed in the United States of America

Library of Congress
Catalogue Card Number
94-79217

ISBN 1-878208-50-0

CONTENTS

Dedication

This book is dedicated to my best friend and wife

Ermajean,

and our two children,
Fred Tucker, III and Lucinda Ann Kirk

and

To John Wallace, Bob Houk, and Joe Boleman,
my loyal partners for four decades.

Preface

Call it what you may! It started out in my mind as the story of the Tucker Company, but soon became interchangeable with my own story. So it's an autobiobgraphy of both me and of the company.

Suffice it to say that it seemed to roll off the end of my pen and the next thing I knew it became a challenge to continue, and fun to complete. Most of it has been done in the quiet environs of the Library in Naples, Florida. Any inaccuracies this book may possess in finished product can be charged off to the sun and the clime of an area we have visited and considered ourselves a part of since 1958.

"Best wishes"—which is the way I have signed nearly all of my letters for now over four decades!

/s/ FCT, Jr.

July, 1994

FAMILY BACKGROUND

"The challenge in life is to decide what's your major aim—to be rich, a successful golf champion, world's best father, or what. Once that's settled you can get on with the happy, orderly process of achieving it."

Stanley Goldstein.

We are all greatly influenced by parental guidance and family life, and also by unplanned happenings, all of which combine to make up one's life's story. I am no exception.

My mother was born in Winchester, Indiana, one of two daughters of a loving, educated mother and an attorney and Indiana Appellate Court judge father. She graduated from DePauw University in 1909, met a fellow student, my dad, while there, marrying him in 1910.

Dad was brought up with an older sister and a younger brother in meager circumstances in Hume, Illinois (population 492). He was influenced greatly by a wonderful mother, but had little contact with a rather distant father. Dad graduated from DePauw in 1908, working his way through all four years and becoming a legendary all-time athlete of the school. He earned eleven major athletic letters and captained the football, baseball and track teams in hls senior year.

My father and mother lived in St. Louis and Memphis, a couple of years in each place, where Dad coached athletics and taught English and mathematics. They then moved to Cincinnati, with Dad working for two years as a salesman for the Aeolian Piano Company. My late, wonderful older (by twenty-two months) sister Emma Gene was born there in 1916.

My parents moved to Indianapolis, returning to many DePauw friends, in 1918, the year I was born. It was 1918 that Dad started the F. C. Tucker Company. We lived at 926 Fairfield Avenue in a half a double for one year and then moved to home ownership at 3231 College Avenue, where we lived for the next twenty years.

Emma Gene and I went to P.S. 76 at 30th and College and went on to and graduated from Shortridge High School, which we later learned was one of the ten best high schools academically in the nation.

My own grade school class was skipped twice (2B and 4A) as a group, as we always believed because our legendary principal, Miss Belle Ramey, was the aunt of our beautiful classmate, Margaret Ramey. Good contacts create interesting results.

Ours was the only single family home in the 3200 block on the east side of College Avenue. The others were doubles or duplexes and thus had rented tenants often coming and going. Our home, where we lived as a family of four for twenty years, was a two-story frame house with a large open porch across the entire front. There we sat on summer evenings, with Mom rocking back and forth in a huge porch swing. I always sat in a chair because the rocking swing made me dizzy and uncomfortable.

It was on that very porch one afternoon in the late summer of 1936 that the Dean of Freshmen Men from DePauw paid me a visit. I had been accepted at Dartmouth College in New Hampshire, and I was headed there in two weeks, when the affable dean sat on that porch and reminded me that my parents had met at DePauw. That made me wonder if Dartmouth really was where I should be going. The dean was an excellent salesman, and I soon realized that perhaps my Dartmouth judgment had been a bit hasty. Neither Mom nor Dad had ever resisted that decision of mine, but I didn't suppose that visit from the DePauw dean was accidental. Anyway, two weeks later I enrolled at DePauw as a result of a fateful afternoon visit on that College Avenue porch—and just look at the extra train fare I saved my parents by not going off to Dartmouth!

But back to my childhood. Inside our home and slightly to the left was a stairway ascending to a landing, from which one turned right to reach the second floor. To the right of the front door was the living room, behind which was the dining room and through that to the left was the pantry and kitchen, reached also from the landing by a back stairway.

The dining room stays particularly in my memory. That is where Dr. James Carter, our family physician, caught up with my short legs

2

and vaccinated me for measles and smallpox under the dining room table — much to my chagrin. It was an incident which for years didn't particularly endear the medical profession to me. A funny thing though, speaking of childhood doctoring, I never minded going to the dentist because another family friend, Dr. Karl Kizer, dentist, sat me in his chair, let me play with the instruments and made me believe that a visit to the dentist was always going to be fun. At least he didn't have to chase me before we got started.

The pantry and kitchen were Mom's domain and rather a constant place of work. What a wonderful cook she was! That kitchen saw continuous family activity. Our dog, Rocky, for example, after he got hit by an automobile out in front of our home was encased in a leg cast during his fortunate recovery and carried into the kitchen. I made it my business to sleep on that kitchen floor beside him for several nights in a row, and together we got him back to normal.

Upstairs we had three bedrooms, one bath, and to the rear a sleeping porch which became my own bedroom during most of my early years. My single bed was handed down from my paternal great grandmother, and as I think back on it now, I believe it was as hard as a rock. But I had a lot of privacy and a room only a step or two from the bathroom, which was an advantage in early morning hours during the school years. Rows of windows back on that sleeping porch gave me a lot of daylight. When my friends would come to awaken me to go to the tennis playground on an early Saturday morning, I would tie a string on a small dinner bell and hang a weighted end out the window to ground level, thereby allowing my wake-up friends to arouse me with slight tugs on the string. In this manner they could let me know it was time to get up and out before the rest of the family was awake. A glass of milk and a cookie on the way out the back door was enough to get me started those early mornings of youth, and we were always the first group on the courts. I'm not certain what happened to my tennis game (no instruction!) but I did enjoy those early morning wake-up matches.

My parents' bedroom was across the hall from the bathroom to the south rear of the upstairs, and my sister's was to the south front. The third, or guest, bedroom was to the west front and later became my own full-sized room by high school days. But I never lost a fondness for my sleeping porch "eminent domain," where each night before I would fall asleep I planned for big things for the days ahead. Ours was a happy home and each one of us respected and loved one another—and of great importance I believe a day never went by without one or all of us interjecting some sort of humor into the family day.

In my memory our back yard looms large. It went back to the alley alongside the detached two-car garage. One's perspective changes as he/she grows older and now that square of grass would surely appear very small. I know that's true because the grade school classrooms of School 76 really did seem small when many years later I went back to the school.

Produce wagon vendors and ice-men came through our alley every weekday, and a wooden ice-box on our back porch was filled every day or two with a fifty or one-hundred pound block of ice. It melted each day into a large pan below the ice-box for daily disposal. We had a coal furnace, with Dad carrying the ashes to the alley every so often as part of his weekly chores. Mom did the laundry and ironing in the basement, and I recall her as always busy, always singing as she worked, a happy soul who spread cheer wherever she went.

Dad drove to work in either a Studebaker or a Chevrolet, and anytime he bought a new car we all exploded with excitement. Automobiles didn't cost so much in those more simple days, but the dollars were hard to acquire and bought a lot of value. I still can remember the wonderful smell and odors of the new car to this day.

Life was generally less complicated. Things were slower, and there were fewer complex pressures. All, or nearly all, of our city's people were law-abiding, hard working, frugal, and generally polite citizens.

Mom and Dad built their wonderful dream home on Lot No. 1 in Avalon Hills in 1940. To this day that lovely brick colonial home, consisting of four bedrooms, den, four-and-a half baths, maid's quarters, and a three-car garage remains in our family, since son Fred and daughter-in-law Becky bought the home from Mom's estate some ten years ago and have raised their two youngsters there since. Incidentally, the home with all of the finish details cost less than $20,000, including architectural plans and supervision in 1940. Now over fifty years later, it is still a charming home, a reminder of the joy the home brought to Mom and Dad. They had started out together as a newly married couple nearly forty years before without much in the way of assets, so it was a symbol of their joint achievement.

I still often drive by that "home of memories" on College Avenue and feel very fortunate for having lived there all of those significant years of my life. I remember our Thanksgivings and our Christmasses with our relatives from Winchester present, and I can still see our neighbors and their houses as I recall them then and now. We didn't live ostentatiously, but we were comfortable and happy and always had a houseful of friends from high school and college days coming and going, with our home a headquarters of fun and friendship. My best friend in those days, Bob Springer, lived at 3200 Broadway just one block through to the west, and we beat a path back and forth daily as we grew up together, became Eagle Scouts together, walked to school and back together, and shared many fun times together. Bright, handsome, promising Bob was one of the first to join the military in World War II. He had just graduated from Butler University when he became an Army pilot. Bob was tragically killed on a test run over Bolling Field in Washington, D.C. when an engine failed, causing a crash into the runway from which he had just taken off. When he was killed I was with the Navy in San Diego and unable to attend the services. I still visit his grave at Crown Hill from time to time in memory of our long and valued friendship, and a time on College Avenue in the days before things grew complicated.

Everything and everybody must have a beginning for how else do we ever reach an ending? —Anon.

Let's reminisce about Indianapolis, capital of the State of Indiana, in my pre-teen years, before the move to Avalon Hills. The city was thriving and growing with a population of 350,000 people. Life was serene, not hectic, and full of fun-filled pleasures which didn't cost very much to enjoy.

Our street, College Avenue, ran north and south. In the 3200 block where we lived for twenty years, from about 1920 to 1940, we were but some three blocks from the north edge of the city, which was pretty well identified as Fairfield Avenue. Street cars went up and down our street, north and south, and ran from Fairfield Avenue south some three miles to Massachusetts Avenue, thence southwest to Pennsylvania Street, and on south to Washington Street, just one block east of L. S. Ayres Department Store, where everyone went to shop.

Street cars provided the bulk of transportation in those days in all directions from downtown. In summertime they featured open sides with foot platforms for all to enjoy the cool breezes in warm weather. Safety rules were not that rigid. We would sit out in front on those late summer afternoons and watch the homeward bound passengers, some riding to the next stop, but others just hopping off at their most convenient location. I remember the ladies in colorful dresses and hats and the men with their heads mostly covered in the light staw hats which you seldom see any more. The street car fare was ten cents per ride. Weekly roundtrip books were a dollar and a half, and transfers to an adjacent line cost just two cents.

We knew everyone in our block, and I can still remember most of their names and their homes. Our grade school at 30th and College was brand new when I started, and my older sister and I walked back and forth each day with our neighbor friends. A highlight on weekends in good weather would be to walk to the Nick-Kerz Company Department Store just above Fairfield on College, where we could "just look" and not have to buy. That store, two floors and a basement, looked huge in those days. It now stands forlorn, in total disrepair, and as I sometimes go by, it looks like many a wonderful neighborhood small store all over America now long forgotten and long forsaken.

I got my first haircut at Fairfield and College. Judging by its length now I must have really gotten my parents' monies worth! If memory serves, the price of haircuts was raised from 25¢ to 35¢, much to the temporary consternation of all.

As time rolled on and as we edged closer in age to high school, the town continued to grow with its expansion along College Avenue reaching 38th Street, and then 42nd Street. That became more than just a casual walk. My good and longtime late friend Ben Weaver and I rode our bikes to McCammon's Drug Store at 38th and College one Saturday and splurged on a 25¢ chocolate malted milk apiece. Just west of McCammon's during our high school years was Eaton's Restaurant, where all of us would go after movies or high school parties and where our folks could all call genial Walter Eaton, owner and proprietor, who could immediately say,—"Yes, Mr. Tucker, Emma Gene and Bud are here with their friends and I am sure will be home soon." Walter knew all of us and watched over us as teenagers just as if we were his own!

Our downtown in those days also had movie houses—Apollo, Lyric, Indiana and Circle Theatres—and two other main, fine department stores, Wasson's and Blocks, both like Ayres, owned and operated by prominent Indianapolis families. Our tallest building downtown in those days was the twelve-story Merchants Bank Building at the corner of Meridian and Washington Streets (then known "throughout the civilized world" as the Crossroads of America). The Tucker Company sold that building many years later in 1977.

Commerce, industry and real estate were all growing and thriving in the mid and late 1920s and Indianapolis was developing into a fine, stable residential community of prominence in the Middle West. Politically we had the usual two party system, with such fine public servants as Mayors Lew Shank and Reg Sullivan, a Congressman who was in Washington, seemingly forever, named Louis Ludlow, such United States Senators as Sunny Jim Watson, Albert Beveridge, Bill Jenner, Sherman Minton, Vance Hartke and Birch Bayh among others, and four U.S. Vice Presidents, Schuyler Colfax (1869-73), Thomas Hendricks (1885), Charles Fairbanks (1905-09) and Thomas Marshall (1913-1921). The latter four were the last Hoosier U.S. Vice Presidents to serve our nation until Dan Quayle's election to that post in 1988 as a running mate with President George Bush.

For recreation and fun in those early days we all went to Broad Ripple and Riverside Amusement Parks. Broad Ripple at 6200 northeast was really out in the country as a last stop on the street car. Riverside was at West 30th Street and White River—a long walk from the end of the street car line in that direction. Roller coasters, ferris wheels, arcades, skating and dance rinks and all sorts of food items were always available at such places. Each September around Labor Day we would all go to the Indiana State Fair (I still do and have *never* missed!) to repeat many of those same exciting amusements. By high school days we had all learned to drive, and some of the more affluent of our friends would even have cars, usually second-hand. When I first borrowed my parents' car I could buy a gallon of gas at the Standard station at Fairfield and College (northeast corner) for 18¢!

A fellow named Pop Spencer built a popular drive-in named The North Pole at 56th and Illinois Street during our high school years. Many a summer night we drove in circles around and around "The Pole" stopping occasionally for a coke and a hamburger, total 50¢ plus 10¢ as a tip for the pretty waitresses, just to "see and be seen." And speaking of cars and driving skills in those days, I had a friend named John Brandon from Boy Scout Troop No. 80, who lived with his physician father and mother at 32nd and Meridian Streets. They had an electric automobile which John was allowed to drive on Friday nights. All of us took turns as passengers. The driver steered the auto with a series of handles, sitting in the left rear seat while the three passengers sat in each of the other three corners of the square cab facing one another. The ceiling was high, the windows large, and the strange feeling of whirring up and down Meridian Street to the astonishment of onlookers was an unforgettable experience.

We could go to the games of the professional Triple-A baseball team, the Indianapolis Indians, but that was it for professional sports in those days. We didn't have a downtown arena or stadium, we didn't have a downtown medical center and campus, and we didn't have nearly 1.2 million people, city and county combined, as we do now. And life, except for those difficult Depression years of the thirties, just seemed to go along and grow and people seemed to obey the laws and live peaceably with one another. We lived through the John Dillinger days (he came from Mooresville, just southwest of Indianapolis, and robbed his first grocery store on West Washington Street), and we survived the Ku Klux Klan days led by one D. C. Stephenson. The notorious "Steve" went to prison in 1926 at the hand of Prosecutor Bill Remy, a close friend of my parents, who received national fame for ending that insidious movement in our city.

And yes, things did grow and people came and stayed in our city and developed a pride in who and what we were and are. And their families and their sons and daughters have also stayed and continued a commitment to one of America's great cities - my home town!

I entered a body of 3400 students at Shortridge High at age twelve with dripping-wet weight of 110 pounds liberally distributed over my 5' 4" frame. The first day I lost my locker combination and whereabouts in gym class and had to call Mom to come and get me with additional clothes since the ones I had worn to school were locked in my gym locker. I announced I'd never go back to that big school, to which Mom agreed. I then was firmly transported back there the next day at her command and direction.

Those were the days of the Great Depression and our family wasn't immune to its problems. I remember Dad getting up in the middle of the night to walk around the block, worried of course, but never quitting. He used to say that no one could describe those days of turmoil without going through them. He had an offer to work in site location for the Sinclair Refining Company at $600.00 per month (a princely sum then) but turned it down to keep the Tucker Company afloat with effort, hope and persistance. I've often wondered what would have happened had he accepted that offer.

Times gradually got better and Emma Gene went off to Bradford Junior College in Haverhill, Massachusetts after her Shortridge graduation. Two years later, at age sixteen, I too graduated from Shortridge and went off for a one-year post graduate study at Lawrenceville School, a New Jersey prep school. It proved to be the best learning experience of my life, although the start was a bit "bumpy" when I confronted courses in physics and trigonometry. I scored 47 in my first physics exam (although I slept on the text book the night before at a fellow student's suggestion), and fearing that I wasn't doing much better in trigonometry, I hastily switched to French and U. S. History, realizing that with a high school diploma already safely in hand, it would have been rather embarrassing to flunk out there in a repeat of the same grade level.

Fred C. Tucker, Jr.

Tucker Talk

Measure your talents and abilities early on and don't jump into the water without an advanced course in swimming and survival.

A Lawrenceville professor in English proved to be the best teacher I ever had. He taught me the eternal value and importance of our own language, both in written and spoken form. It remains a "thing" with me to this day, and to see letters go out or be received without attention to grammar and mechanics still mystifies and challenges me nearly every day. We must insist on excellence in the English language.

Emma Gene entered DePauw as a Junior and I began as a Freshman in the Fall of 1936, after the porch swing talk I've referred to earlier. A true, favorite family story tells of Dad sitting us both down in the living room before we left for Greencastle that Sunday afternoon, saying: "You will both go through rush down there at school and your Mother and I want you both to make your own choices, but assuming you will be invited, you need to know that I am going to pay house bills *only* at Alpha Chi Omega (Mom's DePauw sorority) and Delta Tau Delta (Dad's DePauw fraternity)!" Luckily each of us did as directed, and that's the pledging pattern that occurred, much to our eventual happiness.

Tucker Talk

Don't ever lose sight of the appreciation of the valuable things in our life and be loyal to the source of the means to pay for them!

Both of us were active in all sorts of activities at DePauw, as we both had been at Shortridge, and the friendships formed at both schools have been enriching and invaluable ever since.

Emma Gene graduated from DePauw in 1938 and enrolled at the Ray School of Photography in Chicago, a nationally known and excellent photography school. My parents were intuitive in that choice for her. As matters developed, she had a wonderful artistic flair for photography and eventually had a wedding and portrait studio of note in Indianapolis. After her marriage to Mr. Robert Hall of Boston and New York, Emma Gene owned and operated two successful studios of commercial, fashion, and portrait photography in New York City, first on upper Broadway and then at 34th and Madison in Manhattan. She was in the "big leagues" by then and had many a national magazine cover to her personal credit after that.

Some more comments about Emma Gene and Bob Hall. They were married in November, 1946, a month after our son, Fred III, was born. Bob grew up in Boston, one of two sons of a high school principal. He summered at Dennis, Cape Cod, Massachusetts, graduated Phi Beta Kappa from Harvard where he lettered in track and high jumping, went off on a fellowship to Oxford College in England, and later joined Bache and Company (now Prudential-Bache) in New York City. There he eventually became vice chairman and treasurer. He came to Indianapolis as Commanding Officer of the U. S. Naval Armory in the last year of World War II, and it was here that he met Emma Gene Tucker, later to become his wife.

Emma Gene and Bob first lived at 23rd and Fifth Avenue in New York City, across from Norman Vincent Peale's Marble Collegiate Church, in a third floor walkup apartment (eighty-seven steps and no elevator). They later bought a lovely apartment at E. 67th Street and Lexington Avenue, where Bob still resides as a widower to this date.

Their marriage and great careers—he as an investment banker and she as a professional photographer—literally took them through the years around the world. After he had taken early retirement from Bache and Company, Bob became head of Orion Pacific, an investment banking house, and they lived in Hong Kong for five years of a continually exciting life. Emma Gene by then pursued her photography more as a hobby, but wherever Bob went, she and her camera and talent were always close by.

My sister and brother-in-law bought a beautiful 1790 remodeled home on ten acres adjacent to New Milford, Connecticut, during those days, and while the Halls were in Hong Kong the lovely landmark caught fire and burned to the ground. They set about rebuilding it some months later; it became a show place in that area, replete with pool, guest house, and a completely rebuilt and beautifully furnished main house carefully patterned after the initial plan.

In the early 1980s Emma Gene suffered a mastectomy, and although her condition seemed to improve, the cancer ultimately spread. In spite of an heroic battle carried on with her usual indomitable spirit and optimism, she died an untimely death in New York, on July 14, 1985, at age sixty-nine. There was never or ever will be another Emma Gene: captivating and imaginative, with a tremendous personality and vital sense of humor. She probably had more friends than anyone I have ever known except for our mother and my wife. She is buried alongside our parents in Crown Hill Cemetery in Indianapolis.

But let's return now to my DePauw graduation—June 1940. Off I went to Harvard Law School for a year before becoming a guest of Uncle Sam and the U.S. Navy during World War II. I wasn't a very good law student and never developed the patience to become a lawyer anyway. Still, courses in "Contracts" and "Real and Personal Property" did serve me in good stead in the years which followed.

In early 1942 I was commissioned an Ensign in the U.S. Naval Reserve, was assigned to the Office of Naval Intelligence and was sent for first reporting duty at the Zone Intelligence Office in Cleveland, Ohio. Upon arrival there I joined a group of some fifteen other newly commissioned officers led by a commanding executive officer who was a Navy career individual.

Shortly after being acquainted with our responsibilities, I received orders to report to Naval Intelligence Headquarters in Washington, D.C. where I spent eight weeks in training conducted by instructors in domestic intelligence from the Navy, the Army and the FBI. It was a fascinating and new experience to learn the involve-

ments of the gathering and handling of classified information helpful to the national war effort. We learned the tracing and following
of individuals in mock exercises, the method of acquiring information from total strangers, the reasons for retention of useful intelligence information, and the practical acquisition and handling of
information deemed either confidential or top secret in character.

One particular class taught by FBI leadership has always remained with me, for it taught the unforgettable message that "we were
to never trust anybody," made necessary by the information-gather-
ing needs of our war efforts on a national scale.

I remember being assigned to teams of three and four individuals who spent days at a time in mock surveillance, the following of
"planted" individuals who were always trying to elude us by bus or
taxi, or were ducking in and out of buildings in efforts to lose us or to
cover their tracks. We learned (and this stays with me to this day)
that you can walk up to a stranger or a group of strangers and ask, for
example, "what did that fellow you were just talking to say or discuss?" and invariably, without hesitation, you would get an immediate answer even from a total stranger. Try it for the fun of it, and you
will be surprised how open a reply you will get. Also in those days
the busy and crowded Western Union offices were ever present, so
we learned by following our "quarry" that a written message for send-
ing could be completely discerned by grabbing the pad upon which
he just transcribed a message and seeing the imprint left on the succeeding blank page.

I went back to Cleveland at the end of the course and became
involved in domestic intelligence assignments in the northern forty-
four counties of Ohio. We were seldom in naval uniform, traveled in
plainclothes garb, carried identification credentials, and conducted
literally hundreds of background checks upon individuals about to
be assigned to either confidential or secret billets in the U.S. Navy.
We learned to go into the individual's hometown, get a transcript of
performance at his or her high school, visit with teachers there who
could reply to the individual's reliability and competence, and then
go door-to-door in the residential neighborhood where the individual
had lived to gather insights. All of us would be surprised how much
our neighbors know about us. How freely, both good or bad, infor-

mation would come out during such conversations! We submitted dozens of written findings on investigated individuals to Ninth Naval District Headquarters, and although not privy to the results, we could tell reasonably well whether the individual was going to get the contemplated assignment or not.

One particular Friday we received a call from a local Cleveland citizen about a conversation overheard in a restaurant the previous evening, which he deemed damaging to our U.S. war effort. An individual in a Navy officer's uniform had been telling others at his table that he was on leave from carrier duty in the Pacific. He said he was just returning from a secret aviation mission over Japan, which had emanated from his ship's flight deck.

My executive officer, one Jack Williamson from Lake Charles, Louisiana and a young lawyer by training, and I "went to the records." With a meager description of the individual provided us by the informant, we were led to believe that the offending party was likely to be a regular Navy officer-graduate of Annapolis. We traced a possible candidate by searching age groups and records and identified a regular Navy lieutenant from Lorain, Ohio. We then took a chance on calling him by telephone, learned that he was indeed on leave, and made an appointment to meet him at a certain downtown hotel lobby in Lorain the following Sunday. We had guessed that the incident to which the officer had referred in the restaurant was the famed Shrang-ri-la Jimmy Doolittle raid over Tokyo. The source of the bombing U.S. Army planes had never been publicly revealed of course. And our suspicions proved correct.

Jack and I put on our white Navy uniforms, headed for Lorain, and met the individual in the hotel lobby as planned. Into the coffee shop we went, thereby creating an informal and quiet atmosphere. Jack, who was an excellent interrogator, took over the conversation. Yes, the individual said, he had been with a group of friends in that particular restaurant that night in Cleveland, but certainly had engaged in no damaging conversations. Jack, ever patient and probing, affirmed that our suspect had indeed been appointed to Annapolis a few years before. Jack kept asking who was with him in the restaurant, what all had they talked about. Finally he told him what a concerned Cleveland citizen had told us he had heard and reported to us. Continued denial of the accusations by the individual only seemed to increase Jack's patience and persistence. Finally, worn out with the questioning and quite obviously highly agitated, the individual broke down and cried, admitted he had talked out of turn, probably trying to impress his group of friends, and acknowledged that he should have known better. Our written report sent off to headquarters the next day undoubtedly was an unfortunate end to a naval career. Again we never were advised of the outcome. We felt sorry for the individual, but we had a job to perform, and we both learned a lifetime lesson on the value of confidentiality.

Too many times since have I seen many examples of the "folly of loose lips." As a matter of fact, I learned from an individual in real estate in New York City that the beginning of several major real estate happenings of his occurred when he overheard the conversations of strangers in his office building elevator. These people should have been listeners and not talkers. A person need not be mysterious in dealing with others, but he must know when and how to keep confidences of vital importance to the matter being worked upon.

After fourteen months in the Cleveland assignment, which involved many other similar incidents, I realized that I was gaining an advanced degree in the skill of people-handling which would serve me well in all the years ahead. Five of us then received orders to go to the Henry Hudson Hotel in New York City, where we were enrolled in another eight-week crash course in Operational Intelligence. Naval Intelligence had taken over that hotel for training. I had another course in "people handling" within the Naval service eventually, a course both interesting and invaluable. From New York I was sent to San Diego, where I became the Naval Liason Officer with and at the Coast Guard Air Station across from Lindberg Field in San Diego. I made dozens of daily flights down the Mexican coastline with my new Coast Guard PBY flying boat friends, and carrying out coastal patrol and observation duties with them. They were all accomplished fliers and enjoyable companions. Captain Burton, the Commanding Officer of the San Diego Coast Guard Air Station (it's still there!), would call us all together in his quarters on most days that were fogged in and we would be his guests at a poker table with lunch served to each in rather grand style. You see, some duties during the war were not entirely without fun and relaxation.

After a few months I was transferred to the Naval Operating Base at Long Beach, California. I learned a lot about the ships berthed there, of all shapes, sizes, and descriptions. Soon I was to join the staff of Admiral Kincaid, head of the Seventh Fleet "somewhere" in the Pacific. I embarked from San Francisco aboard a troop ship with some fellow Naval officers and thirty-four days later after crossing the Pacific, via Honolulu, arrived at Samar, Leyte, headquarters of the Seventh Fleet. Days and nights were spent on watch duty. Curiously enough, on one of my night watches I was present when the Japanese message (their code having then been broken) detailed their sighting and sinking of the cruiser USS Indianapolis. That dark page in U.S. Naval history, when an unprotected cruiser was viciously attacked and sunk, should never have been written.

We later moved as a unit to the old Polo Grounds in Manila, joining the staging preparation for the planned invasion of Japan. Fortunately, the war ended and the Japanese were defeated and brought to surrender as a result of the atom bombing of two of their major cities.

But of utmost importance to me, while I was an Operational Intelligence Officer at the Naval Operating Base in Long Beach, California, I met and married the lovely Ermajean MacDonald of Pontiac, Michigan. We were introduced to each other in Los Angeles, where she was visiting with three other young ladies from her hometown. We went together no longer than ten weeks and were married in Pontiac, Michigan on September 2, 1944, to the probable dismay of her parents who hadn't seen in-law-to-be up to that time. Enroute to Pontiac and the wedding, Ermajean did go to Indianapolis to meet Mom and Dad, but her fine parents, Erma and John MacDonald never laid eyes on me until two days before the wedding. I guess that was par for the course in those days of war and uncertainty, but I doubt that we as parents would have been very enthusiastic in a like circumstance, had the roles been reversed.

We were married in the Episcopal Church in Pontiac with Norine Isgrigg, Ermajean's sister, as Matron of Honor, and my lawyer cousin, Bob Oliver of Winchester, Indiana, as Best Man. Other close friends were detained by Uncle Sam: Bill Welch aboard the

U.S.S. Indianapolis in the Pacific and Bob Morgan as a U.S. Air Force flight instructor at Ocala, Florida, were thus "unable to make the formation."

We stayed that night, now fifty years ago, at the Statler Hotel in downtown Detroit, and bearing sufficient gas stamps, returned to naval duty driving back to California via Lake Tahoe. Our first apartment was on Leimert Boulevard in southwest Los Angeles, about a mile or so walking distance from the Los Angeles Coliseum. Those were the days in which no real worries existed, though my meager naval pay left us close to broke at the end of each month. But we ate out, entertained friends, and somehow made ends meet, a good warm-up for the years to follow. Incidentally, I should have said that during our brief courtship, sister Emma Gene happened to come to Los Angeles for a visit. You can imagine an "Emma Gene" and an "Ermajean" both in the same room and how likely it was with so much in common that they would hit it off thenceforth! I am sure that Emma Gene softened the shock for my parents with "Little Buddy" about to get married to someone they had never even met!

Tucker Talk

Be willing to accept all of the help you need when you need it and never, ever, have a short memory!

As I have said, we were based in Leyte, moved to Manila, and helped to set the stage for the invasion of Japan. President Truman, in his carefully considered judgment, ordered the dropping of the atomic bombs, which action brought a hasty conclusion to a conflict which otherwise would have exceeded the D-Day carnage in northern France some few months earlier.

Our unit went by air from Manila to Honolulu. There Gene Pulliam, now Publisher of the *Indianapolis Star* and *News* and a long-time good friend, managed as an officer in the Port Director's Office to get us squeezed aboard the Argonaut, U. S. Navy Communications Flagship, for a return by sea to San Francisco. Crowded in a berth aboard a train to Chicago and thence to Indianapolis, we were finally dispersed to our various homes, once again safe and sound with our loved ones.

CHARLES JEWETT   FELIX McWHIRTER   CHESTER JEWETT   FRED TUCKER

Cooperation

Further proof of the unfailing cooperation between the school and those who have graduated from its halls is to be had in the fine response made by some of the schools former athletes to an emergency that arose during the last football season. With Coach Buss incapacitated by a nervous breakdown, and with the big Centre game staring the football artists in the face, things were in a bad way.

The situation was saved by the arrival of Charles Jewett, Mayor of Indianapolis, Chester Jewett, his brother, Fred Tucker and Felix McWhirter, all of Indianapolis who immediately took charge of practice and training. All four men are wearer's of the "D" and showed the teams some stuff which they used to work on their opponents. The work of these men kept the team in good trim during the absence of Coach Buss and they all look glad enough for the opportunity to get into the uniform again and work for "Old DePauw".

19

Sister Emma Gene, age 6, and Brother Bud, age 4.

September 2, 1944. Just Married! Bud and Erm in Pontiac, MI.

Mother and Dad in the mid 1950s.

(Top) Jaycee radio program in the 1950s.
(l-r) Tom Keller, Chuck Brownson and Bud Tucker.
(Bottom) Dad's staff mid 1950s. (l-r) Bill Christena, Sales Associate;
Katie Froney, Secretary; Mary Smartz, Bookkeeper;
Thelma Hickman, Office Manager.

FORMATIVE YEARS AND MY START IN REAL ESTATE

"Judge a man by his questions rather than his answers."
Voltaire

Now just what was I to do? What was I educated and trained for? Whither should I go? What did I really want to do? I was no different from millions of other young, discharged service people—all confronted with the dilemma of finding identity and future after a time in which most decisions had been made for them.

One fellow naval officer I met along the way was named Herb Naper. This tall, gangly, fun-loving and bright guy who hailed from Chicago convinced me that if we went into the oil business at any level we could be millionaires by the ages of thirty. My recollection is that I went to try it ahead of him and at that point we must have gotten out of touch. Ermajean and I headed for Tulsa, Oklahoma, where I applied for work in the Land Department of the Stanolind Oil and Gas Company, part of Standard of Indiana, and a "small organization" of some 35,000 employees! I began to work with oil and gas leases in that part of the country and was doing well enough that one day my boss called me into his office to tell me that I was being transferred to Biloxi, Mississippi. I remembered several foot-soldier Army friends who had marched in the mud in Biloxi during training, and I knew then and there that I should politely ask for a few days to think it over!

About this time, as though Heaven-sent, (and I surely have always believed in such things) my dad showed up in Tulsa to spend the night with us. He said he had been in Kansas City on business and just thought he'd come on down to see how we were getting along. I didn't sense his planned purpose at the time, but as he left the next morning to return to Indianapolis he put some literature on the entry hall table, indicating that I might want to read it. I did so, resigned at Stanolind, and enrolled immediately in Real Estate Appraisal Courses I and II about to commence the following week at the Uni-

versity of Tulsa. There is a lot to timing in life, as we all find out sooner
or later.

Ermajean was by then pregnant with Fred III and so headed back
to Indianapolis to stay with my parents while I went to school in practical real estate appraising for six solid, intensive weeks. The courses,
taught by nationally known practioners, were divided into residential and then non-residential aspects of the profession. The curricu-
lum involved field work, practical examples, night studying and
difficult written examinations set out by the American Institute of
Real Estate Appraisers. All of this work was calculated to lead to a
professional designation after many years of further practical experience. I can still remember what professors Schultz and Montana and
local Tulsa experts, Messrs. Collins and Grant looked like and how
they taught, and the inspiration that they provided to a class of some
forty ambitious young men. And as the years went by, I played a lot
of golf with Bob Collins, a 4-handicapper from Tulsa who was more
my dad's age, and Tom Grant, Jr., my own vintage, who eventually
became President of the National Association of Realtors, as did I.

What a happy and unusual introduction to this field of real estate which was to become my life's work! And what a smart dad I
had! He never ever told me what to do but he provided the opportunity for my own personal choice. All this time he was backed fully
by my mother, who quietly helped direct my many moves and who
was the smartest lady I have ever known - and that takes nothing
away from wife, sister, and daughter, all of whom are smarter than I
am anyway!

Tucker Talk

*Always be open minded and inquisitive, ready to seize oppor-
tunity. For the curious mind asking questions, answers will
be provided in curious ways never imagined!*

After the successful conclusion of the Tulsa courses and exami-

26

nation, I knew that I was headed for a career in real estate back in Indianapolis. But I've always been thankful that I tried the "oil business route" first because I would have never been satisfied had I not.

Dad knew all along that I'd wind up in real estate and so did Mom, although neither of them ever said so. However, once I arrived in Indianapolis, my father said that maybe I'd like to start out learning the business with another mentor. He suggested his close friend, one of the deans of Indianapolis real estate, Paul McCord. I replied that I'd rather make mountains of mistakes right there in the F. C. Tucker Company instead of being embarrassed with such inadequate knowledge elsewhere. Dad agreed and started me out in residential real estate brokerage. "That's where you start to learn where things are, who owns them, how to find ownership at the courthouse, and otherwise become self-educated by asking questions and searching for answers, Bud," he said.

I've often said that I learned the real estate business in the wrong climate, because, in effect, post-World War II was an era which was too easy! The hardest thing to do was finding a listing—a house to sell—for veterans returning from War in an atmosphere where anything offered was sold almost immediately. A practical lesson in the law of supply and demand ensued, because little or no product was created during the war years and there was suddenly more demand than existing supply of properties could provide. Our own case is a good example. We worried about where we would live because there were so few places available. Luckily Dad was a tract developer and home builder. One of his recently built, two-bedroom homes became our first purchase for $7500, via the G. I. Bill of Rights with a low downpayment and 4% interest. Location: 3302 North Colorado in Tucker's E. 34th Street Addition. Another thing Mom and Dad wisely did—they made *us* buy the house and eventually gave us a new electric refrigerator (and that was all!) as a house-warming gift. That refrigerator lasted twenty-five years.

My pay at the Tucker Company was a draw (not salary) of $35.00 per week and the rest was up to me, with Dad often saying that "the sky is the limit on what a real estate commission saleman can make."

"But Dad", I'd say, "where's the product?"

So out we went and he showed me how to get a listing. I believe the address was 5900 Allisonville Road, but I can't remember the price—probably the mid to high twenties. It was a fine three-bedroom stone and frame ranch home at a competitive price for those days.

And so it was time for my first home sale experience. We advertised the home with a brief description, got six immediate calls and I sold it in two days for the full price. What a salesman I was, out there shooting fish in the proverbial rain-barrel. Back I went to the office, all excited. I put the purchase offer and acceptance on Dad's desk. He looked it over and then looked up at me saying, "Don't I remember that those sellers are getting a divorce?"

I said, "Yes, but I got her signature on the acceptance part. The house is sold, sold, sold!" He frowned. The wife finally got the ex-husband-to-be to sign up but I'll never know what other concessions she must have had to make to atone for her acceptance without his consent. The trouble was that her real estate salesman was as naive as she was.

Tucker Talk

Get every interested party on the dotted line before you calculate the commission. You may, however, breathe a silent sigh of relief when you know that the sellers, no matter the circumstance, have to sell!

Well, I must have made some more sales, because we were able to keep up our house payment. But prior to all of this and of much more importance, on October 22, 1946, just three days short of my own birthday, Fred Tucker, III entered our world of joy and took over bedroom #2 at 3302 North Colorado. Ermajean proved to be a wonderful, loving mother and also expert repairman: between baby feedings she bored a hole in the kitchen floor to drain the melting ice in our wooden ice-box down to a tub in the basement rather than letting it spill over her constantly polished kitchen floor. I am sure that each time Mom and Dad came by to see Fred III enroute to the driveway and their car, Ermajean paraded them through the kitchen by the wooden ice-box. Voila! A new electric refrigerator from the display at the annual Indianapolis Home Show appeared. And General Electric to boot! We used to sit and stare at it contentedly while eating supper in the evening.

About this time I joined the Indianapolis Jaycees, as had nearly all of my returned veteran friends from high school and college days. We had a wonderful group of over five hundred members weekly "learning civic service through constructive action" as the national Jaycee creed goes. Those few years of Jaycee membership would prove to be of enormous influence in my life in many meaningful ways. I became program chairman during my second or third year of membership. We met weekly at the Washington Hotel's sixteenth floor, and it was my pleasant duty to arrange weekly programs and, with my committee, to obtain weekly speakers, and in most cases to introduce them to the group at each meeting. This made me learn to organize my thoughts and speak on my feet, an experience which was to serve me well thenceforth. I ran for president as a petition (non-selected) candidate. Shortly thereafter, I won by four votes, in a spirited contest and campaign culminating on election night at the Athenaeum and attended by over four hundred voters. And this, as much as any one event, probably contributed to the ultimate growth and success of the Tucker Company! Later you will read why I - and we - owe so much to our experience and involvement in the Indianapolis Junior Chamber of Commerce—and all without design or plans at the time whatsoever!

THE GROWTH YEARS

"The highest reward for a person's toil is not what he gets for it, but what he becomes by it"

John Ruskin

At the time of my Jaycee presidential campaign, one John Wallace was executive vice president of the Indiana Junior Chamber of Commerce. At the same time, Bob Houk ran for secretary and was elected that same election night at the Athenaeum. Little did I know at the time that these two fellows, later joined by one Joe Boleman, were to become my equal real estate partners and close, close friends for the next forty years! These three individuals were at the very heart of what the Tucker Company became, and it was at this time we came together.

John Wallace, "tall, dark and handsome," at that time in his mid twenties, was born to a medical doctor and his wife in Lynn, Indiana. After his father's untimely automobile accident death, John moved with his mother and his sister, Sue, to Richmond, Indiana. John became a celebrated high school basketball forward at Morton of Richmond High School and soon found a basketball scholarship awaiting him at Indiana University. His college career, though, was interrupted by World War II, where he served as a B-17 navigator for thirty-five missions over Germany. After his return from the war, John became a leading Big 10 scorer for the Hoosiers, with a record which stood the test of time for another ten years after his graduation. Lovely Sarah Lukemeyer, daughter of a family practice physician from Jasper, Indiana, and also then an I.U. student, became John's bride shortly after graduation. Together they became the proud parents of five youngsters: Jane, Martha, John, Lu and Andrew, who have all continued as credits to the Wallace clan. Unfortunately, some seven years ago, wonderful, lovely, fun-loving Sarah contracted cancer and died an untimely death in Indianapolis, missed by all her friends.

Fred C. Tucker, Jr.

John was about to "go on the road" for the Modern Fold Door Company of New Castle, Indiana, when I intercepted his thoughts and plans, suggesting that he come over to join my dad and me in the real estate business. The attraction of staying in Indianapolis appealed to both Sarah and John, and thus a new real estate career was born. Ironically, John had accepted an offer from a friend who knew not much more about the subject than he did.

Almost simultaneously Bob Houk came into the picture. Bob and I had known each other before the War at DePauw University, but not as well as we later did as fellow Jaycees. An excellent student and native of Alexandria, Indiana, and the only child of Lillian and Glen Houk, Bob was awarded a Rector Scholarship at DePauw. There at the university he proceeded to distinguish himself as student and campus leader. A classmate from Evansville, Indiana, the lovely (and still lovely) Marion Pfitzner became Bob's bride upon their graduation from DePauw. Bob then joined the U. S. Navy and became a commanding officer of a Navy sub-chaser with duty in the Pacific Ocean area. After the war Bob joined Walter and John Holmes as a salesman in the oil business in Indianapolis and environs. He and Marion have been blessed with a son, David, and a daughter, Julia (Julie), both of whom also became DePauw graduates. They lived on Kingsley Drive in Indianapolis, and when we fell into conversation about the sale of their home for a move to larger quarters, Bob told me he, too, had been approached by Modern Fold Door. We talked and he agreed to come on board at the Tucker Company shortly thereafter.

And so, the three of us started to learn real estate much like the "blind leading the blind," but with expert guidance from my dad. About this time another fellow named Joe Boleman showed up at our office doorstep in the Peoples Bank Building. Joe and his younger brother Ben were natives of Indianapolis. They were the sons of Attorney Edward and Mary Boleman, and lived in the 4700 block of Park Avenue. After graduation from Shortridge High School, Joe went to Wabash College and following Marine Corps officer duty in the Pacific, transferred to and was graduated from Indiana University. He was joined at IU by his new bride, attractive Martha, who as Martha Casey was one of four daughters of medical doctor Casey and his wife of Huntington, Indiana. This union was blessed with two fine daughters, Ann and Polly, both of whom have helped to add lustre to our "Grandchildren Group" along with the Wallace Five, the Houk's Two, and Ermajean's and my two youngsters, Fred and Lucinda, of the Tucker Tribe.

How did we find him? Handsome Joe came in one day to see and visit with the now "veterans" John, Bob and me and gave us fifteen minutes of the greatest sob story of all time. He explained that he was making $400 per month as a National Cash Register salesman and that he and Martha with their two little girls lived in half a cramped double on Winthrop Avenue. Almost with tears in his eyes he told of two-year-old Polly's birthday party in that cramped backyard just that past Saturday. He said, "I just leaned over that rickety backyard fence and said aloud, 'Little Girl, I'm not giving you the opportunity you deserve!'" We all three were impressed. Joe left, after asking us to respond to his rather desperate sales inquiry. Then John, our eternal stand-up comic quickly said, "I don't know whether he can read or write, but after a story of real baloney like that let's don't let him get out of our sight."

And then for the next forty years we became as one - four equal partners, four young men with varied talents, and four young men eager to learn and eager to excel - and yes, eager to try it together in a real estate market that would see many changes. Joe, too, had been an active Jaycee and as the years rolled along many people referred to us as, not the F. C. TUCKER COMPANY but the J. C. TUCKER COMPANY—obviously and luckily for good reason.

Joe always went out the door in the mornings saying "I'm going out to sell such and such a house" where most would say "I'm going out to show such and such a house." Viva La Difference! Stories abound for forty years, but one of the first and greatest was Joe Boleman's first sale—and John could tell it best of any of us.

Out Joe went to sell this particular home we had listed on Broadway Terrace in north Indianapolis. After being gone a couple of hours, back he came and put a purchase offer in the full asking price upon John's desk for his further handling with the home's owner. And John, after reading the document said: "Joe, congratulations, but you have the wrong street address on the offer! The house is on the other side of the street!" And Joe's retort: "John, that makes little difference—the buyer knows where it is, I know where it is, and the buyers have just bought it! How much is my first commission?" The sale was closed! That sale was the springboard for the nearly daily friendly jibes that John aimed at Joe for at least the next thirty years. Joe, always unperturbed, just kept that winning smile always on his face and with Gary Warstler proceeded to build the largest and most productive residential sales organization ever seen in all of Indiana. With continued growth since Joe's regrettable death some three years ago it has thus remained—a real tribute indeed to a wonderful guy who knew each sales associate's name, that of his or her spouse, the names and whereabouts of their youngsters, his or her concerns and triumphs, and certainly each one's loyalties and many fine accomplishments. It was Joe, Motivator Joe, who insisted on company parties, picnics, trips, and gatherings—and upon recognizing excellence in the company annually. Joe's Recognition and Awards Day normally lasts between three and four hours, and it fires up motivation, employee satisfaction and pride in our company.

Good people bring good people. These three partners of mine continued to recruit and attract strong people with abilities similar to their own until we became a group of some twenty-five strong! Dad was of constant help to the four of us and always encouraged our growth and the fun we were having with it. We often recall that he was the one who pulled us back from the end of the diving board just as we were about to go off into the deep end.

Tucker Talk

Respect your elders, learn carefully from them, and never, ever have a short memory!

The company continued to grow a bit in both personnel and volume. For example, the residential division alone has gone from approximately 20 associates in 1965 to 450 in 1993, with the dollar volume of residential sales increasing from nearly $12,000,000 to $863,000,000 during those same years.

We realized how important it was to have products on the shelf—listings, if you please in order to serve an expanding clientele. And then one of our fortunate breaks occurred which served to convince us that good and conscientious service would become our hallmark and important reputation. Bob Morgan (of the fine law firm of Smith, Morgan and Ryan) represented us in all legal matters. This was logically so, for Bob and I, who had known each other well since high school days, continued as friends through DePauw, Harvard Law School, War service and return to civilian life. Bob is two years older than I and possesses a keen legal mind sprinkled heavily with a unique and lasting sense of humor. He had grown up in the educational world, went through Tech High School where his father, Dewitt Morgan, was principal and later Superintendant of the Indianapolis Public Schools, graduated from DePauw as a Rector Scholar and completed with distinction requirements for a degree from Harvard Law School. After entering the practice of law, he became an Army pilot and instructor in Alabama, Florida and Arizona and at war's end returned to his law firm and practice in Indianapolis.

Among his many clients was the Western Electric Company, which had just built a large manufacturing facility at East 21st and Shadeland in Indianapolis. Bob called one day to say that Western Electric was going to move some three hundred families from their Hawthorn Works in southwest Chicago and that he felt that we could represent most of them in home purchases in Indianapolis.

What a "bonanza" for a real estate firm anxious to grow and serve in our great community! We literally set up informal shop in the lobby of the Graylynn Hotel at 11th and Pennsylvania Street, since razed, and arranged to meet and handle the housing needs of most of these families who were newly billeted in Indianapolis by Western Electric.

Thanks to Bob, Western Electric leadership in Indianapolis recommended us for the home purchases of these new employees, and our lives became quite busy and indeed quite productive.

Our major problem as a young, growing residential firm was lack of product, however, and it was evident that we would have to rely on our fellow Realtors who had the listings while we had most of those buyers. We made a public vow then and there to all of those local competitors, most of whom proved friendly, that someday when the tables turned and we had the products we would lend full coopera-tion then for and with all of them as repayment for their help.

I well remember that John Wallace pulled in my driveway one Sunday afternoon to get names of prospects, a list of offerings, and a city map. With full confidence away he went to successful results, even though he was still learning the streets and locations of the homes offered for sale by our competitors. The Western Electric newcomers were and are wonderful people, and many of them be-came our friends as the years elapsed. Two stories of many, however, depict our continued learning experience. One day John had an engineer and his family going with him from house to house, and as they would leave one home heading for another, John noticed that the engineer family head was always last to leave each home while others in his family waited in the car. Finally John went back into the house they had all left and saw the man spinning a silver marble across the living room floor. John, being a competitive athlete, asked the man if he wanted to shoot some marbles with him. The fellow unabashedly said, "John, how else will I ever know if these houses have settled?—and when we find the one where the marble goes straight we will buy it!" John refrained from asking whether the fellow's wife's opinion would matter. Suffice it to say the couple did buy an "unsettled home"!

Another experience with those nice people was one of my own. I had spent a full, ten-hour day with a Mr. and Mrs. Novak, only to have a call the next morning from a voice saying "This is Mr. Novak and we are here to look for a home." I stammered for a moment and then said "Excuse me Mr. Novak, but don't you remember that we were together all day yesterday?" He laughed in response and then explained that a Slovenian family name of Novak is like Smith, Brown and Jones in America. "Bud," he said, "you will soon meet many more of us by the same last name when all of us from the Haw-thorn Works arrive. Even though most of us aren't related, you'll have to learn our first names or learn to count us off by numbers." I got it all straight. They bought homes and couldn't have been nicer people.

Now it seemed that we were off and running. Bob and I stayed downtown with my dad, starting to learn a bit about commercial and industrial real estate. John and Thelma soon joined us, and Joe along with Gary Warstler moved the branch office to 52nd and Keystone in quarters four times as large. Downtown for us by then was Suite 810 in the then new Indiana Building at 120 East Market Street. Here we had moved in the year 1955 to a bit less than 1,000 square feet of "New Headquarters space" for the F. C. Tucker Company.

Appropriate now are some brief comments about the history and occupancy of the Tucker Company in the Peoples Bank Building, next door east, at 130 East Market Street. That downtown site was the founding location of the Tucker Company, selected by my dad way back in 1918, some thirty-five years before the move to the new Indiana Building. The McWhirter family not only owned the Peoples Bank Building, and still do, but also headed the Peoples Bank, and still do. Dad served on the Peoples Bank Board in later years and had a long and close friendship with Felix McWhirter, head of the Bank, and L. Roy Zapf, the Bank Counsel and Board member dating back to DePauw days when all three of them were students together.

When the four of us joined the Tucker Company in the late 1940s and early 1950s, headquarters was on the seventh floor of that building. Walter and Maude (husband and wife, last name unknown) ran the sandwich stand in the lobby. Cookie was the mailman and Ollie the elevator operator. The latter two had some proclivity for John Barleycorn. The fact that the mail was often mixed up by delivery to the wrong floors and the cage elevator in Ollie's practiced hand seldom hit the exit floor evenly seemed to add lustre and fun to our daily activities. Dad was a good sport after all of those years to move to a new building next door just to satisfy the desires of his new young real estate associates, who preached, "Look the part if you are going to be the part!"

Miss Mary Smartz, Secretary and Bookkeeper, and William Christena, master commercial salesman, were Dad's only associates until we came along, and both couldn't have been nicer to newcomers than were they. Bill Christena died with his boots on at eighty-two, Miss Smartz retired after over twenty-one years of loyal service, and after the legendary Thelma Hickman took over and helped us with our growth. Thelma's effervescent humor and piano-playing talent saw us all through many a crisis. She went thirty-seven loyal years before calling it quits herself. Now happily married, she is still in close touch. We will always honor Thelma Hickman for her part in our company's growth. Incidentally, in those early days Miss Smartz would always pay each of us our earned commissions in cash from a small brown envelope, but I guess we modernized in time and finally started being paid by check.

My dad died on Memorial Day, May 30, 1958, at the age of nearly seventy-one. He was playing golf at Hillcrest Country Club, which he helped found, that day with his usual foursome and became ill on the sixteenth green. Tommy Vaughn, the pro and long-time respected family friend, tried to take him to the hospital, but Dad insisted on driving the short distance home on his own, where he went into the house and stretched out on the couch in the den. Mom went to the kitchen to get him a glass of water, and when she returned he was gone with a fatal heart attack.

Ermajean and I had spent that day with friends at the 500 Mile Race. When we returned home that afternoon to our home at 5402 North Delaware, we saw John Wallace sitting on the ground in the side yard. He came over to meet us and quietly said "Bud, you lost your dad this afternoon and I'm here to help." John took us out immediately to be beside Mom, who typically grieved about the loss my sister and I had just suffered even though we were, of course, full adults and on our own.

Dad was one of a kind: patient, bright, self-made, modest, a wonderful husband and father, and an inspiration to all who knew him. He loved people, he was a master salesman, and he cared about what happened to others. It is difficult for anyone to measure from whence came his or her strengths and attributes. But whatever strengths and attributes I do possess, I was blessed with two wonderful parents who shared their talents, beliefs, and ambitions equally with me and my sister.

The services for Dad were most appropriate, with those who came out of respect for his memory legion. The eulogies came from both our minister and from the DePauw University President Russell Humbert. Dad had by then served as University Trustee for several years.

Two things said to me during those visitation times at the mortuary have always stayed with me, oddly enough, and I have remembered them and quoted them to others many times since. One family friend, outspoken and direct, said "Bud, just remember that there's not a damned thing you can do about it!" and the other, perhaps more gentle, comment from another family friend went like this: "Always remember in a time of grief and need that your friends form a strong circle around you and will never, ever let you fall!" Two good things to remember in times like those.

At that point the promise I had made to John, Bob and Joe took immediate effect, and we became equal twenty-five percent partners from then on in all we did for better or worse. The first step the new partnership took was to gamble the opening of the first Tucker residential branch office. Ermajean was the one who spotted the vacancy at 5410 College Avenue, and that first of several branches to follow became a reality. John agreed to organize and manage it and was smart enough to take Thelma Hickman with him as his assistant. The two of them doubled as stand-up comics for all of the years that followed, and before long they had some sixteen people under their wings selling north and east-side residential real estate. The office had one half-bath and a rear entrance which on hot days provided air conditioning (they just left the door open). All those who labored there enjoyed that little office and can still recall the fun and certainly the trials that followed.

John still says to this day that his biggest problem was fending off newcomers whom Bud would meet over a weekend and send into John to hire and train on Monday. He said if a guy just smiled or said hello to Bud in church on Sunday he was told to report to John the next day. Needless to say none of them and I mean none ever worked out and thus a potential career of mine in what they now call "Human Resources" was nipped soundly in the bud! (Bud!) Finally John said one day—"Bud, do me a favor, don't go anywhere this weekend and don't talk to anybody! I just need a breather!"

If any four people had more genuine fun building a business than we did I don't know where they are. In those formative years, for example, "Women in Real Estate" was a subject seldom discussed. They did not at that time seem to have the experience or training which the profession demanded and which they were later to so successfully demonstrate. To make a point with which we then agreed, John often told the story of a closing he had arranged for 2:00 P.M. at 5410 College where he represented the seller and a "lady-broker" represented the buyer. The papers were ready and revised over and over, while John watched the clock. Finally, at 2:45 he turned to the lady broker with his own sellers anxiously present and said "Madam, just where are your buyers?"—And she replied: "Oh migawd I knowed I forgot something!"

Later on, as is well known, ladies came successfully into the business, into the Indianapolis Real Estate Board, and into our Company and in 1993, eight of the top ten residential producers in the Tucker Company were—you guessed it—WOMEN! Bless them all. We as men show houses by saying "this is the living room and this is the dining room" while the women Realtors say "this corner is where your lovely piano will go and just imagine that settee over there by that beautiful bay window!" And all men must remember that it's always been the women (wives) who buy the houses and its the men (husbands) who pay for them! (Until recently, when two-income families mean both are paying!)

In the early 1960s and through attending meetings in Chicago and elsewhere of the National Institute of Real Estate Brokers, I met a man named Ned Spring from Minneapolis, Minnesota. Knowing that he had a real estate organization in Minneapolis much like the one we hoped to have some day, we asked for, and received, an invitation from him to visit there and see his operation in action. A few of us flew up there for a two-day visit and were impressed with how he had departmentalized the business into residential, commercial, industrial and management. We noticed particularly his strong real estate advertising program in the Minneapolis area. But the thing that struck all of us most visibly was his slogan in all of his advertising of "Ring Spring" done with a clever logo showing a typical home telephone line crumpled into the letters of "Ring Spring." We learned from him the importance of a slogan and a logo and saw their effects in action, measured by his very strong sales results.

We returned home and met as a small group in our backyard the following Saturday to discuss "Slogan and Logo" for the Tucker Company. To this day we aren't certain who "thought it up" (Erma–

jean says she did and some think our longtime, close General Out-door Advertising friend and leader, Bill McMurtrie, who was present that day, did) but suffice it to say that "Talk to Tucker" was born that morning. What a wonderful, lasting, fortunate happening for all of us, because it worked, and it stuck!

That morning in 1962 nimble minds present said our signs should be shaped in a "Block T." They would be in yellow and black, because the highway people said that these are the most recogniz-able colors. We would put them out late on a Saturday night with no prior publicity or announcement on all of our residential listings, which by then had become more than a respectable number. And "sure 'nuff" on that fateful weekend the city woke up to "Talk To Tucker" (in hand-written logo) signs just all over everywhere in our market areas! The reactions were terrific and well beyond our wild-est dreams. It is doubtful that any one thing has helped our remark-able growth more than that sign and slogan, since copyrighted by lawyer son, Fred Tucker III, who is now the Tucker Company presi-dent. Remember that the sign says nothing about "for sale" or "for lease" and doesn't even mention real estate. But it has proven over and over and over that it is a motivator and an action propellant! The logo has become nationally known and respected and even has helped the identification of our great city in a lot of visiting minds. I have had foreign letter-questions and comments, one from Ger-many, one from Italy and one from France even asking "what does it mean, because we saw it in your city while visiting friends and rela-tives!"

As a final comment, we have been told by nationally recognized advertising and public relations people that our sign, logo and say-ing "Talk To Tucker" is by far the most singly recognized such sales aid in the State of Indiana!

Tucker Talk

Identify and respect the most important single things at-tached to your growth and success. Support time-tested slogans, colors and logos and count your blessings when they have been powerful tools. Our people, who are the

*other equally strong reason for our success, deserve the
continuation of the Tucker logo as a strong sales ally and
any change would do nothing but confuse the public,
which represents a third leg of our successful stool!*

Now a little bit about two other strong reasons and forces responsible for our growth—and in no particular order. Just thirty years
ago we realized in our growth and future needs that we needed a full-
time financial accounting officer who could marshal our resources,
organize our financial wherewithal and keep us on a solid financial
track commensurate with our careful image-building of successful
growth and service. The CPA firm of Ernst and Ernst sent us one of
their young associates named Roy Altman. Roy proved through the
years that followed to have the unusual combined strengths of talent, qualification, and loyalty we so badly needed.

He was in his late twenties, a native of Pennsylvania, and a
graduate of Penn State. As we were to find out later, Roy was a former
Penn State golf team member with a four-handicap, a fact not looked
on lightly by most of our Tucker Team! Roy's growth and maturity
through the years have been astounding. With all due respect, most
accountants are not "people people," but Roy proved to be the opposite! Roy Altman is an accountant with a sense of humor, great
people skills, and an innate ability to charm the most hardened
banker. The entire financial community knows and respects him and
his talents reflect well on the continued direction of the Tucker
Company. And although he supported growth and risk-taking, some
of these risks didn't help Roy's sleepless nights on various occasions.
His career has been distinguished.

Gary Warstler, Senior Vice President, and a Residential Man
for All Seasons, is perhaps our most unheralded hero. A great and
long-time friend in real estate and a brilliant guy named Bill Jennings
called one day again nearly thirty years ago and said "our mutual
friend, Lee Warstler, whom we all know at the Indianapolis Country Club, has a talented, energetic son, Gary. Lee thinks Gary be-
longs in real estate. Since you folks are growing more than we intend
to in our building and land business, why don't you talk to Gary?"
Thanks are due to Bill Jennings for his sound advice.

Joe and I met with Gary, and as though it were pre-planned, Gary joined Joe. As much as any one person in our company, Gary Warstler organized our residential branching, growth, system, training, advertising, and managerial selection for the future. He and Joe devised a most remarkable co-manager system. They stressed careful selection among their sales associates, insisting on two co-managers of exact opposite characteristics for each branch office. It has worked like a charm. Without exception, among what must now be some twenty-five or thirty co-managers, you will see a more quiet, reserved, well-organized person keeping close to the branch office and seeing to the "details." Meanwhile, his or her counterpart, invariably a gregarious, outgoing, cheer-leader type, goads and commands, pushing, consoling, and needing to be reined in "for a rest" once in awhile by his close friend, associate and co-manager.

The Tucker Company is part of an informal national network of excellence in the profession. There is a group of several real estate organizations around the nation affectionately known as "The Dozen," all of whom are much like the Tucker Company in significant ways. Gary has been their president and commands the respect of all of them. Being involved with The Dozen, Gary, who has an unusual bent for comparative statistics, both locally and nationally, is able to measure the Tucker Company's performance and convey it statistically to the public. I often discuss with him the repetitition of statistics telling of the company's achievements. "Won't a lot of people be offended if the company constantly reiterates its stenghens? Would a bit more modesty be more becoming?" He tells me as a good, long-time friend that such pronouncements help his people and bring business to our doorstep. And then I often reflect quietly on what my longtime good friend, Bob Walker, one of the smartest individual real estate practioners I've ever known, said one day to me, to wit: "Bud, always remember that unfortunately the public demands bigness!" How true, and yet in so many ways it is true that it is unfortunate!

Gary has never elected to be a part of Tucker Company ownership. He has the unusual talent of remaining in the background, while he and (now) Jim Litten quietly and effectively plan their next moves.

Amusing incidents always happen in any business, and ours has had no exceptions. One day outstanding Susie Hudnut and John

Stewart, two active broker associates, attended a broker's open house together. These events, hosted by a listing broker either in the Tucker Company or one from another group, occur frequently by prior announcement. All who care to attend briefly do so to view a product for which one of these representatives might have a buyer. Normally the host broker provides some refreshments or light lunch as a friendly inducement for attendance. On this particular occasion, Susie and John drove to the appointed address and walked into the designated home through the unlocked front door, noticed the refreshments and decided to tour the upstairs of the home first. Following their inspection, they were confronted at the foot of the stairs by a lady indignantly asking who they were and why they were interrupting her luncheon bridge group. She threatened to call the authorities for help. Susie and John, mouths open, apologized profusely and realized that the broker's open house was in fact next door. I've often wondered if some weeks later, knowing them as I do, they went back to again apologize but really to learn if the lady would possibly offer her home for sale in their capable hands. If they did and she agreed, you can bet those two live-wires made another sale.

Tucker Talk

So, if it's possible, turn a negative into a positive with politeness and persistence!

And while I think of it, here is another one that has stood the test of time. A few years ago I earned the nickname of "Towbo" in our Tucker Company expanded family. It goes back to those few days some winters ago when Indianapolis was visited by an almost paralyzing ice and snow storm sufficient to stop business and commerce hereabouts for a better part of a week. My habit was to get to the office "no matter what" almost daily. So in I went only to find very few others "dumb enough" to have ventured out.

Having little else to do, I set about calling our various branch offices only to find that most of their telephones were going unanswered. And then I thought, "Wait a minute! Incoming telephone calls are our bread and butter, and if we are going to 'be the best' we had better sure as the dickens show it!" So the first of the next week I sent out a memo "to all hands" expressing to them the hope that all were well and had survived the ordeal. But at the end of the memo I suggested, "henceforth, no matter the circumstance, please remember TOWBO—The Office Will Be Open—TOWBO! You had better believe that I would have done well not to send the memo, but look at the fun they have all had since, saying, "How's old TOWBO today."

During the years we dealt with many interesting and often well-known people, but perhaps the most famous seller of all was Miklos "Mickey" Hargitay. Mickey escaped in the late '50s from Budapest across the Alps into Switzerland and thence into Canada where Ross Christena, youngest son of my dad's associate Bill Christena, sponsored his entry into the United States. Mickey knew no English, was in his early 20s, was a handsome 6´ 2″, two hundred thirty pound young man full of ambition and pleasant personality.

Ross was a devoted attendee at Hoffmeister's gymnasium in Indianapolis where he introduced Mickey to the finer points of body building on a strenuous regimen. To make a long story short, and as is well known, Mickey developed a body which ultimately led to his becoming Mr. Universe in London not too many years later.

In order to get Mickey started in some gainful occupation, Ross purchased two residential lots in the Forest Manor area and Mickey, an absolute artist with his hands as carpenter, plumber, electrician and painter, personally designed two small bungalows which he then built by himself, by hand on each of these lots. Ross saw to it that we had the listing and sale of the two homes and by then all of us were becoming well acquainted with a young man who not too much later was to become internationally known both as a body builder and as a Hollywood movie star. I believe John took charge of the sale of the two homes because he lived close by at 36th and Grant Streets. Of all things, we soon discovered that neither house would qualify for FHA financing because, in each instance, the bathroom was placed directly across the hall from the kitchen. Mickey, in broken English and always pleasant, explained to us that in his country the kitchen and bath belonged together because family meetings always took place each evening in the kitchen amidst servings of beer, wine and other liquids destined for elimination close by. Mickey seemed to make me his point man during the listing period and would always call in to the office with a friendly question of "Bud ist dere?" John seldom has called me on the telephone ever since with any other greeting than that! Incidently, Mickey built his body to such a point that he could balance his beautiful two-year old daughter in a standing position upon his right hand and arm at a moment's notice. The child, Mary, was the proud product of Mickey's marriage with his first wife, Mary, a handsome, young Indianapolis native lady. As his career progressed, the marriage unfortunately went by the wayside.

In any event, in 1961 Mickey returned from Italy where he and his then new wife, Jayne Mansfield, had just completed filming *Samson and Deliah*. Jayne had gone on to California and Mickey stopped in Indianapolis to greet old friends and attend the 500 Festival Ball. His locks were still at shoulder length from the movie, but when he spied Ermajean and me across the ballroom floor, he made a dash for us. He embraced us and continued the friendship and good looks for which he was always known.

We explained to him that evening that we would soon be heading for the west coast with Fred, age fourteen and Lucinda, age twelve, for an automobile trip out to California and back before they had to return to school. Mickey immediately produced a pen and paper, wrote down his address and telephone number in Beverly Hills and insisted that we call upon him and Jayne upon our arrival. Naturally, we did so and had an unforgettable experience. When we drove up alongside the house and got out of the car, we looked down over the fence and saw Jayne in a pink bikini lounging alongside a heart-shaped pool, busily talking on the telephone. The house had formerly belonged to Rudy Vallee, and Mickey had completely remodeled it, by hand, into a real work of art. Mickey greeted us at the door, took us down around the pool and introduced us to Jayne, who proved to be nice and friendly, and genuinely interested in us as a family. I proceeded to take several color pictures of Ermajean and the youngsters around Jayne, and we still have slides of that incident plus some of Jayne and Mickey that day as well. Upon our return from the trip, we made it a point to mix those slides among the regular ones of the trip and would let them come on the screen, unannounced and unidentified, as part of the "trip showing" to friends. Needless to say, those pictures got everyone's attention and still do.

Although we have lost touch with Mickey, who still lives in that area, we know that he would recall our friendship as genuinely and effusively now as then. We must indeed look him up again sometime and learn of all that has happened in his life since that day some thirty years ago.

Today the Tucker Company has some twenty offices throughout metropolitan Indianapolis and indeed the State of Indiana. It continues to be the dominant leader in real estate in Indiana with a complement of over 1,000 associates in all phases of real estate: residential, commercial, industrial and management divisions. This is a far cry from some twenty-five years before, and is a tribute to hard effort and a series of goals which continue to be attained by today's strong and dedicated leadership. We never ever planned to be a certain size but did commit ourselves to professional excellence, the practice of the Golden Rule in all of our dealings, and the familylike treatment of all of our personnel. We have striven for professionalism and I believe we have indeed achieved it!

THE SPICE OF LIFE—THE TAKING OF RISKS

"Don't put all of your eggs in one basket but strive for
variety, the soul of excitement and change."

Anon.

We did practice variety daily in the 1970s and 1980s to a rather
marked degree. Let me recount in some chronological detail various
involvements and happenings.

I suppose it all started with my sale of the famed Marott Hotel
for $3.9 million in 1957. The Marott was a real city landmark hav-
ing been designed by architect Robert Frost Daggett and built along
Fall Creek Boulevard in 1926 as one of the most beautiful hotels in
the Midwest. A friend from New York often sent notices of his schedule prior to periodic meetings of the National Brokers' Institute, of
which we were both members. This particular meeting in early 1957
took place in Washington, D. C. and in preparation I took descriptions of two Indianapolis properties for his study, perusal and reac-
tion. One was the $350,000 seventy-two-unit Dartmouth apartment
building on East Michigan Street and the other was the four million
dollar Marott Hotel property at Fall Creek and Meridian.

Looking over my real estate descriptions, this New York broker
friend advised me to go back home and sell the Dartmouth locally
(which I did on contract and with my commission spread by agreement over five years) and then said that he and his brokerage people,
knowledgeable in hotels, would come to Indianapolis the very next
week to see the Marott.

They were as good as their promise, and their attention to details of the sale showed the work of real pros in action. While my
friend sent flowers and candy to the lovely widow owner, thereby
gaining her sincere confidence, his people studied the performance
and figures of the hotel and prepared an interesting offer. One of their
contacts in Chicago agreed to buy the property, sight unseen, predi-
cated upon a lease-back to a second Chicago hotel operating group
with ingenious terms fair to both parties. The late Neal Grider, Ex-

ecutive Vice President of the Peoples Bank, was the widow's advisor, and upon his positive recommendation, this sale became a reality. Dad, Neal and I went to the Chicago closing some two months later, met with over twenty investors and lawyers, buyers and lessees and watched the carefully orchestrated closing of a transaction which was highly educational for me in those earlier days of my business career. My share of the commission, my biggest transaction to that date, was just under six figures and as much as anything gave me confidence to look further and higher in the myriad fields of real estate brokerage and ultimately development. Incidentally, forty-five years later, that same Marott was just sold by HUD out of foreclosure. It went for $2.5 million, with the new buyer further agreeing to add another $2.0 million in renovation funds with agreement to keep it as an apartment rental property rather than an apartment hotel.

About this time, one C. B. Smith, an Indianapolis native, acquired the Holiday Inn franchise for all of Marion County, Indiana, for $2,500.00 (Holiday Inns were then in their infancy). He had 2.5 acres of ground across from the Indianapolis Motor Speedway, and was going to lose the franchise soon if a new Inn wasn't built by him there within a short period of time.

Dick Stackhouse, contractor, Al Ford, architect, and Bud Tucker, Realtor, agreed to design and build a Holiday Inn on that site, with my arranging the financing package for C. B. Smith as owner. Dick and I went to Memphis just to meet with Kemmons Wilson, Chairman of Holiday Inns. We developed a friendship with him and later on developed with Al and the others three more Holiday Inns in Marion County, always including C. B. Smith as part owner in each of our new packages. The Inns were located at 1920 North Meridian Street, Pendleton Pike and Shadeland Avenue, and Madison Avenue and Thompson Road. Bob Houk and I served as principles in the latter. Dick and I secured the site and rights for the Holiday Inn west of Columbus, Indiana, later built and owned by the Dora family, to whom we sold that site and right. We later traded our Holiday Inns for Holiday Inn stock and thus had liquidity, a situation far different from that of most hotel equities and situations.

About this time we became interested in the need for a new downtown hotel. We ultimately created the Indianapolis Hilton, a four-hundred-room and 525-car, twenty-story facility, the first new hotel in Indianapolis and indeed in Indiana in forty years. This is the brief story of how it happened. I went back to see Kemmons Wilson to tell him that we were going to ally ourselves with Hilton, but wanted to maintain his and Holiday Inns' blessing. I always remember his saying "Bud, you can't be married to two women at the same time." Naively enough we supposed that we were forever blocked from further Holiday Inn involvement, which wasn't really so. The Dora family stepped into the picture, made C. B. Smith their one-third partner in Marion County and proceeded successfully to build, own and manage several Holiday Inns in this area. Meanwhile we traded our Holiday Inns interest for parent company stock. Bob Houk and I bought Dick Stackhouse out (much to Dick's financial benefit and for cash!) and proceeded with the Hilton effort.

We first optioned all of the properties on the south side of West Ohio Street just west of North Meridian Street, right in the heart of downtown, persuaded famed Indianapolis industrialist Mr. Herman Krannert and his wife to buy all of this ground and lease the ground back to our newly formed limited partnership, went to business community leadership for equity funding (limited partnership tax rules before the Tax Act of 1986 was a major inducement for such investors), arranged for Metropolitan Life Insurance Company first mortgage loan financing, and entered into a management contract agreement with Hilton Hotels Corporation to manage the property on a fee basis upon its completion.

The Indianapolis School Board Headquarters building at the corner of Meridian and Ohio Streets was razed during night-time demolition, as were the other less prominent buildings to its west. As winning bidder, the Knutsen Construction Company of Minneapolis built the structure designed by William Tabler and Associates of New York City. Our principal Hilton contact through these many months was Robert Caverly, executive vice president of Hilton, with whom we worked carefully to fine-tune the planned result.

It all sounds in retrospect rather simple, but it was far from it, with a final package of some twelve million dollars involvement including furnishings, fixtures, and heavy advertising and pre-opening expenses insisted upon by Hilton. As an important aside it needs to be noted that unlike nearly all developers in this project and in all others later described herein, we have *never* used any public monies for assistance. Had we done so, as all others did, our debts and our payments would have been unbelievably lighter, and I suppose again that we thus wind up in the "naive column." What we did, however, in each instance was on our own, and I remain proud of it despite the many headaches we could have avoided had public assistance been part of the picture along the way.

I can name several examples of projects created since, in which the city has provided the ground and financing for others. Indianapolis has received little or no return to date from such projects, because of definitions of what constitutes "positive cash flow" in protection of the developers and as "inducements" for the projects to occur. Had we depended on city support, we would never have lost the two Hiltons some twenty painful years later. Under city assistance we would have had little or no ground rent or a cash-flow payment well protected by legal language, allowing for long running room for the project's well being. This is not to say that any other such projects have been dishonest. It just says that our refusal to use public assistance cost us a lot of money and headaches along the way.

And so we, the Tucker Company and a small group of civic leaders, opened the first new hotel in Indianapolis (and Indiana) in forty years on May 15, 1970. What fanfare and what pyrotechnics! The entire Hilton Executive contingent from Beverly Hills, California, including Conrad and Barron Hilton and all other principal Hilton officers and spouses flew in for the grand occasion. An open convertible carrying the Hiltons, father and son, came whizzing east down Ohio Street to cut the opening ribbon. Lunches and dinner in the new hotel took place, with Conrad Hilton and his attractive partner opening the dancing on the final formal banquet night. We all finally went home late but happy that it had finally "happened"!

Lynn Montjoy, a fine young man, was sent by Hilton to manage the property, and he and his lovely wife Rita became our good friends and lively parts of our community. Unfortunately, however, a new, smaller hotel usually serves as a training ground for those moving up in food, beverage, administration and sales. We discovered that a steady stream of newcomers would come in, train, and move on, taking with them management continuity and information base so vitally needed in any hotel operation. And it was no fault of Lynn's that he himself was transferred to become General Manager of the O'Hare Hilton in Chicago. At this point in 1978 we opted to turn the property into a Hilton franchise under our own management.

About this time Bob Houk and I had agreed to buy a 109-unit hotel property at the Indianapolis Airport grounds. We did so, turned it into a Hilton franchise, added twenty-five units and ultimately 160 more - and by then, in the late 1970s, were in charge of a four-hundred-room Hilton downtown and a three-hundred-room Hilton at the Airport—and after various stages of remodeling by the mid-1980s we had an operating total of 658 Hilton franchised rooms.

We tried many managerial ideas and people, but found that our most faithful and loyal one was Bob Meyer, who recently retired from active Hilton management after having been with us for over twenty-seven years. In 1985, with both hotels "tired" and in need of renovation (an ever-present need in the hotel business) Bob Houk and I ("nothing ventured, nothing gained") bought out some of our partners at the Airport property, combined the two properties in one entity and did a very major remodeling, top to bottom of the downtown property. We hired Dale Scott, general manager of the Indianapolis Hyatt (which we had created with others in 1977) to oversee the two properties—and enthusiastically hoped for the success which up to this time had not been our good fortune in the hotel business.

It didn't work. As we saw expenses mount, revenues remain stagnant and new hotels come on the scene in downtown Indianapolis, we were hardly prepared, as were *none* in the hotel business in America for what then followed. In the mid 1980s the worst hotel recession (and yes the same in office buildings, shopping centers and apartments) in the past fifty years hit America. This huge slow down was occasioned by over-building, financing which should in many cases never have been approved, and diminished personal and corporate travel. Hotels everywhere started to have problems in 1986 which by 1990 reached shocking levels of foreclosure, loss of equities, and difficult operating conditions. Monies for refurbishing and refinancing became unavailable in the hotel market, and suffering which still continues is just now starting to be abated. The only real cure, of course, in these situations can come about by limiting new development. No new product is needed while existing, good products are available, and these good available products deserve a chance to catch up.

We tried in vain to sell our Hiltons. Our original limited partners had long since recovered more tax shelter than their original investments, but it is interesting to note that in cases like these some people forget the original purpose and its inherent tax advantages, concentrating only on what was put in in the beginning. In a word, Bob and I were the heaviest all-inclusive two investors of nearly all of the rest of the group combined. When we gave the hotels back to a group of some thirteen lenders in late 1992 by deed in lieu of foreclosure, Bob and I were "stuck" with the very painful, negotiated payoff of a certain part of personal liability. That responsibility had been agreed to by us in 1985 as part of our then-new financing package to buy out some partners and do the required renovations the hotels then so badly needed. As is so often the case, needed support and help in such a time of crisis is nearly impossible to find. The new owners recently have been able to start off with low debt, nearly certain success, and a rosy picture almost tailor-made for them by past history. I hope this viewpoint is not interpreted as "sour grapes," because what they inherited with our two properties were opportunities born of conditions and happenings with which they had nothing to do. We sincerely wish them well and have found them to be fine people who will add hotel credit to our community. It was fun for the most part and many worthwile experiences resulted from this major undertaking.

Tucker Talk

All is not gold that glitters. Sometimes pain and failure result from hard but unsuccessful effort. Risk-taking is not for weak stomachs!

While we were creating the Hilton elements of architecture, land purchases, formation of ownership groups and building and opening the property in 1970, I had a call from Fred Risk, then Executive Vice President of the Indiana National Bank. He asked me to come over for a confidential visit about a potential headquarters move for the Bank to a new and exciting downtown location. Fred always has had unusual vision and was given the new building challenge by the Bank. He outlined his thoughts in confidence, designating the square block bounded by Ohio, Delaware, New York and Pennsylvania Streets as his choice. He then asked me to see if all of such properties therein could be optioned for an "undisclosed principal" and cautioned that all such work could well result in "no result."

So back I went to our office to accomplish the task of securing a sizeable chunk of downtown prime real estate. I enlisted the support and help of Kurt Mahrdt, whose father was the INB President and late Chairman. Kurt, a DePauw graduate and one of my closest younger friends, had come to the Tucker Company with a Master's Degree in Real Estate from the University of Florida and was obviously one of our fast-rising stars. Armed with talent, intelligence and persistence, Kurt without doubt became the best and toughest negotiator in the Tucker Company and was an ideal choice for this new assignment. We divided up the calls which would need to be made on property owners and lessees in that square city block and set about a difficult and challenging task, maintaining always the confidentiality of our principal and all the time hopefully looking to those owners and lessees for our fees if the project ever came about.

Psychologically one of our principal aids, by pure chance helping our efforts, occurred because most of those owners and lessees assumed that for some reason we were going to change the location of the about-to-be-built Hilton Hotel. In any event, we were able to convince two or three recalcitrant owners that stubborness on their parts could well cause the entire undisclosed but important happening to fail. Usually no one wants to be the glaring "bad guy"—finally we had all of those situations under option for the Bank's perusal and action. Of major assistance on square foot acquisition costs was the willingness of the city, under the dynamic and intelligent leadership of Mayor Dick Lugar to offer to close the diagonal, one block stretch of Massachusetts Avenue. The city agreed to relocate some underground sewer and water lines thereunder all for a reasonable price, thereby completing a square city block for an exciting downtown happening.

One morning a few weeks after this time, the Bank officials called all personnel together at 8:00 A.M. and broke the news to them. The bank was going to purchase the entire block and design and build a thirty-six-story office tower as new INB headquarters. The employees were abuzz with excitement and surprise. The secrecy of all of those weeks of effort and planning had been maintained!

Up went the dramatic and beautiful Indiana National Bank Tower, then the tallest building in Indiana. Actually, a total of fifty-five stories (Hilton Hitol and Bank Tower) were both finished and opened within one block of each other in the same year of 1970. Our analysis of the likelihood of Ohio Street's being the ultimate "Wall Street" of Indianapolis had proven correct, and the revitalization of downtown Indianapolis was underway. The Tucker Company became the leasing and managing agents for the INB Tower, moved its headquarters office to that location and ultimately occupied its entire twenty-fifth floor of some 16,000 square feet. This was the beginning of a remarkable later and continuing growth of our new heralded and professional Management Division, then headed so capably by the late Bill Rife and now overseen by talented Bob Kizer.

This relationship with the Bank continued until the early 1980s. At that time the building was sold to JMB Realty of Chicago, which brought in their own leasing and management teams of professionals as the Bank then became a primary lessee of theirs. Bob Houk and I had an offer from the Royal Dutch Petroleum interests of the Netherlands for the very price that ultimately bought the property, but the Royal Dutch officials overseas did not act rapidly enough at their executive level and JMB prevailed. All Bob and I had as a result was the small satisfaction of having set the price which finally prevailed.

In retrospect, we should have followed our own instincts and gone directly to B. P. headquarters in the Netherlands immediately, rather than following the well intentioned advice of our New York counterparts representing B. P. in America and our co-brokers. These advisers told us that the B.P. committee would act promptly in our favor. (Their meeting was delayed over there and our efforts became history, not to mention the strong six-figure fee that Bob and I would have brought to the Tucker Company table.)

Along about this time Dan Evans, a good friend of Bob's and mine and at that time CEO of L. S. Ayres and Company, called us over for another "confidential consultation." It would almost sound as if our business was often "cloak and dagger." Suffice it to say, though, that confidences issued and kept are often the balance wheel for success in a competitive business world, no matter what the company or the subject.

Dan told us that long-established national retail-leader L. S. Ayres and Company of Indianapolis now wanted to enter the discount department store business in our area and thus offered us the opportunity to develop, build, own and lease back to them original units of some 130,000 square feet including satellite stores in different Marion County locations with a new and copyrighted name of "Ayr-Way."

We set out to develop the first four Ayr-Way centers in Indianapolis. These were located at Pendleton Pike and Shadeland, 8100 East Washington Street, 2300 Lafayette Road, and West Washington Street and Interstate 465. All of these facilities were built and opened, and all of their leases were eventually sold to Target Stores of Minneapolis, the ultimate lessor of these properties. Bob Houk became team captain of all of these major efforts and John, Bob, Joe and I became their principal owners. We have sold the Pendleton Pike and East Washington centers and still own the Lafayette Road and West Washington Street centers and discuss the sale of these currently with various prospective buyers. These opportunities have added to our real estate management portfolios as well.

In the mid 1970s John Jewett, effervescent DePauw graduate and a long time sales leader of the Tucker Company, decided that the Indiana Pacers professional basketball team needed to have a downtown home and not to flee to suburbia as many would have it. John's and my parents, all four, went to DePauw together, and thus I suppose I have known John longer than I have anyone in the Tucker Company. John is enthusiastic and highly intelligent, and became our logical team captain for the Market Square Arena project, which the Tucker Company brought into being as general partner.

John optioned the ground on each side of East Market Street at Alabama. He conceived the novel idea of an arena's being built over Market Street atop two pedestal six-hundred-car-each parking garages on either side of the street. He and I went to see the great mayor, Dick Lugar, who also strongly supported a downtown location for the Pacers, and the deal came about with Mayor Lugar's strong support and leadership like this:

There was a quid pro quo, and properly so, for the city to acquire the land under the arena and then build the arena itself atop our two privately funded garages, designed for six-hundred cars each. Mayor Lugar imposed a requirement upon the Indiana National Bank and our own limited partnership group to renovate the city block on the south side of Ohio Street between Delaware and Alabama with new structures to replace the old, thereby dramatically increasing the real estate tax revenue for Center Township and the city of Indianapolis.

This we indeed did and by 1975 the Bank created a twenty-story office building of some 275,000 square feet on the corner of Delaware and Ohio Street. As a significant addition to the downtown skyline, the structure became known as the Gold Building — an instant success. A 520-car, self-park garage immediately east of the Gold Building followed, and some short years later the balance of the block saw the creation of the 2 Market Square Center, a building of another 250,000 square feet, also a success in terms of rather immediate occupancy.

The Gold Building, interestingly enough, is now owned by the Metropolitan Life Insurance Company in partnership with some seven Japanese banks though the leasing and management of it still continues in the hands of the Tucker Company's Leasing and Management Division. Our Company Management Division has grown to a sizable entity, with responsibility for a total portfolio representing owners of 7.6 million square feet. This ranks the Tucker Company now second in portfolio size in the State of Indiana behind the Duke Company, whose portfolio is largely composed of properties of their own development and ownership.

The Spice of Life

The Market Square Arena story exhibits dramatically what our company in concert with others has been able to accomplish in terms of real estate tax increases for our city during the 1970s and 1980s. A conservative estimate of such replacement of old for new would likely show twenty times more annual real estate taxes enuring to the benefit of our city and its Center Township. This was never set forth as a goal, but was the dramatic happening and result of our efforts, in effect demonstrating that old axiom and challenge of "paying civic rent for the space you occupy."

After the building was completed, our sub-tenants then became the Indiana Pacers NBA basketball team and the Indiana Racers, a professional hockey team owned by a Nelson Skalbania of Canada, who brought a seventeen-year old hockey-to-be star named Wayne Gretzky to our city for Wayne's first professional hockey experience.

The planning, design, and opening were tremendously exciting, and the arena even hosted the Final Four NCAA finals therein in 1981. That tournament was won that year by the Louisville Cardinals. But later, in the darkness of night, Nelson Skalbania packed his bags and left town, abandoning some of his local investors without a team to show for their support and investment. And there we were as general partner with one tenant, the Pacers, and no professional hockey team. We were able to keep going with garage revenue support, but had to find a buyer for our arena and a professional basketball team. Few to this day in our community can recall our position, involvement, and exposure, but John and I with others did find Dr. Jerry Buss of Los Angeles, owner of the Forum and the Los Angeles Lakers who took our place and temporarily saved the day. Ultimately Mel and Herb Simon bought the arena, the Pacers and the garages. "To make the deal stick" the successor-to-Lugar Mayor Bill Hudnut and his advisor-attorney and former Deputy Mayor, David Frick, asked to meet with John Jewett and me at John's home late one evening to discuss our position. The two of us along with several limited partners we had placed in the deal but who were not present were being asked by Messrs. Hudnut and Frick to *give* our interests to the city and the Simons on a "charitable contribution" basis to assure the transfer to the Simons and the saving of the Pacers for Indianapolis! This was one of my toughest decisions of my career, and that of John's too, but we felt that we had to recommend it to our people and we did. The city could have lost the team and the arena could have developed a white-elephant status but for our call. I regret having to have had to call that shot but felt that our commitment to our city demanded it. I went to Herb Simon to try to retain a 10% interest in the deal for our people but was turned down and most of our own people, all good citizens, went along with the sale with a tax incentive but no cash, just out of civic mindedness. The Simons, incidentally, have been good soldiers and owners since, and despite many concessions made to them by the city, have lost considerable monies since there while still holding the team here for our city. But to this day some of our people have never agreed with our decision—and perhaps rightfully so.

It is rewarding at the moment to reflect back on what the general areas of Market Square and the Arena looked like— almost completely dilapidated—some twenty years ago. In 1994 the Indiana Pacers, the Cinderella team of the NBA, played in the finals of the Eastern Division playoffs before capacity crowds at home to the delight of all. But all things change. NBA officialdom has recently declared our arena to be too small, and with a need for luxury private boxes to compete nationally. Not that many years ago we were indeed lucky to create a new arena and have a professional team housed there with only a mediocre record until recently to show for huge combined efforts. The recent spectacular resurgence of our city's team now may begin to justify the faith and hard work many of us have put into the Pacers effort.

Tucker Talk: Never give up when the effort is a good one. Commitment and belief aided by the passage of time will often make you look great, even if sometimes it's just accidental.

What was the next one? Well, the next call came from our friends, Nick Frenzel, Chairman, and Don Tanselle, Executive Vice President of Merchants National Bank. They wished to discuss potential relocation of their headquarters and revitalization of the southwest quadrant of the Mile Square with some major development to be spearheaded by them. The square city block selected was bounded by Washington Street, Capitol Avenue, Maryland Street and Illinois Street diagonally cut through by Kentucky Avenue.

With enthusiasm I called Mr. A. N. Pritzker, legendary Hyatt Hotel national figure in Chicago. I asked for an audience and at his invitation took Bill Moore, Roy Altman and Kurt Mahrdt to the Pritzker apartment on Lake Shore Drive in Chicago for dinner and a meeting with perhaps the most interesting man I have ever met. A.N. Pritzker was in his mid-seventies by then, but still full of boundless energy, and one of the greatest people persons of all time. We talked at length about putting together a hotel, retail and office complex adjacent to our new Convention Center, and then told A.N. about Merchants Bank and its long and successful history. We detailed our association with Mayor Dick Lugar, who by then was nationally known for his intelligence, his leadership, and his belief in the value of public-private partnerships. A.N. came to Indianapolis to meet with the mayor, whom A.N. later supported for Republican U.S. Senator (although A.N. was a strong Democrat). He viewed the site and further discussed the hotel and office complex project.

We appointed our inimitable Bill Moore as team captain of this one. Did Bill ever rise and shine, as Kurt Mahrdt had at the INB project and John Jewett had at the Market Square Arena projects! Imagine my good fortune at being surrounded and supported by such enthusiastic, intelligent and professionally qualified talents!

Bill Moore, Roy Altman and I soon went to Houston, Texas to meet there with A. N. Pritzker and two representatives of the Prudential Insurance Company—Claude Ballard and Bob Lisle. The Pritzkers and Prudential had just completed the magnificent Houston Hyatt. We found while there that A.N. Pritzker was meeting in different suites and times during this same period with similar groups like ours from Cambridge, Massachusetts, Dearborn, Michigan, and New Orleans, Louisiana. Suffice it to say that some months later the

Fred C. Tucker, Jr.

Prudential-Pritzker combine opened Hyatt hotels of various sizes in Cambridge, Dearborn, New Orleans and Indianapolis.

A design team of note from Houston created the Merchants Plaza project for Indianapolis. We were able to get the construction management contract for my long time good friend, Dick DeMars of Geupel-DeMars Construction Company of Indianapolis, ably supported by nationally rated Turner Construction Company out of their Cincinnati office. Bill Moore literally *lived* with the project, nurtured it along, and brought to completion on that key downtown square block a fifteen-story office building of 375,000 square feet, three floors of retail outlets, a 250-car underground garage, and the crowning edifice, a 500-room (largest then in Indiana) Hyatt Hotel. He was again ingeniously aided by the city and Mayor Lugar's commitment to the closing of diagonal Kentucky Avenue to make it all happen. The city has retained ownership of the ground, and unlike most of these public-private enterprises, has received rentals from the beginning for the benefit of the taxpayers. Our city also has gained dramatically from heavily increased tax revenues effected by our joint creation of Hilton, INB, Arena, and now Merchants Plaza projects.

The grand opening of the Merchants Plaza project took place in April, 1977, amidst much fanfare, a formal banquet, speeches by all partners in the new ownership of "P.R.T." (Prudential-Revco and Tucker—Revco being a Pritzker entity). The high point of the evening were appropriate wind-up remarks and observations by A. N. Pritzker, by then a strong friend and a man in his enthusiastic mid-80s. He died at ninety-two a few years ago but left an unforgettable imprint upon all who knew and loved him and upon every governor, mayor, and city wherever he took his Hyatt Hotels. A modest and enjoyable person, he was a brilliant tactician who knew how to make things happen without appearing to be much more than a good listener. His talented sons carry on and continue to expand the Pritzker interests in many ways.

My most recent development effort and excitement became known as the Canterbury Hotel in downtown Indianapolis. Ermajean and I named it after the hotel of the same name in San Francisco from whence I departed to go overseas in World War II. The old hotel we renovated was built in 1928 as a twelve-story hostelry, with two-hundred-small rooms just one block north of the Union Station. The Lockerbie, as it was called, was at that time a handy haven for railroad travelers stopping over in Indianapolis. It later became the well-run Warren Hotel owned and operated by Glen Warren, a prominent Indianapolis hotelier and businessman. Glen also owned and operated the Harrison Hotel across from the Statehouse on Capitol Avenue. After Mr. Warren's death, the hotel fell into less capable and committed hands and was ultimately closed for lack of business and in desperate need of repair and renovation.

It is interesting to reflect upon the dramatic changes which have taken place in the area surrounding the Canterbury since that building was erected. As was already noted, the location of that hotel now nearly seventy years ago was dictated by the proximity of the Union Station, a very active national passenger and freight train hub, just two blocks south of the hotel. Such attractions as the famed Pop June's Oyster House and the Mutual Burlesque Theatre, both on the west side of South Illinois Street between Maryland and Georgia Street, were obvious "drawing cards" for the traveling businessmen who made the Lockerbie Hotel their frequent headquarters. The rooms, some with private baths, rented for $3.50 per night and the food service, dinners featuring steaks and chops in the evenings, were all less than $5.00 apiece.

By the time the hotel became the Warren during the 1940s, most businesses downtown frequently brought their dining and meeting needs there. Visitors were treated royally and fairly, with meals and service costing but ten percent of today's prices. The tradition continues. Famed St. Elmo's Steak House, immediately south of the hotel, still caters to most out-of-town visitors as it has for nearly one-hundred years. Any traveling visitor to Indianapolis who is here for two or three days will likely be directed to St. Elmo's "just south of the Canterbury" for the "best steak in the Midwest" and all usually return during each visit for a repeat performance.

Anyway, it bothered me to come by the old Warren frequently on the way into downtown from the airport, and finally I called upon our "master negotiator" to please get a purchase option on it. I knew Kurt Mahrdt could do it and at a fair price, and he did. Then, with a new-found friend named Don Fortunato of Chicago, we developed an imaginatively exciting hotel plan. Don was one of the founders of the Balcor Company, which he and others had recently sold to American Express and was willing to be part of a Canterbury venture. This project would qualify for historic tax credit once we placed it upon the National Historic Register.

We retained the firm of Morris Nathanson and Associates of Providence and Boston to design and completely remodel and furnish an exquisite, one-hundred room, English-style hotel and ripped out the entire inside of the hotel except for floors, walls and ceilings. The firm created a much-talked about building for our city, a result of which we are very proud. The hotel opened in November 1985. Its grand opening was carefully orchestrated by the talented Peter Neimetz of the Nathanson Company. The Canterbury was dedicated by our governor, mayor, and indeed by the Lord Mayor and his wife of Canterbury, England, all in exciting meetings, luncheons and dinners together. Now, some ten years later, we proudly see the Canterbury as one of only 105 Preferred Hotels worldwide. With his Balcor background and contacts, Don sold several limited partnership interests to help with our financing needs. Quite recently he and I have managed to acquire a favorable new first mortgage loan position which has taken original bond holders out of the ownership entity. For my own part and from the beginning I did give certain minor interests to members of my family and other loyal associates in gratitude for their support of me and my efforts through the years. I believe and know that each of them appreciated that, particularly when small allocated tax breaks came their way before the Tax Act changed such allocations.

I believe the excitement surrounding the Canterbury and St. Elmo's, recently enhanced by plans for the Circle Center Mall, will build to a continuous crescendo until the grand opening of the Circle Center—shops, restaurants, theatres, and famed retail outlets headed by Nordstrom, Limited and Parisian—scheduled for the fall of 1995. Parking above and below ground, enough to accommodate 2,500 cars, will add to the convenience and lustre of the finished product. When the unique "Wintergarden"—an elevated circular glass enclosed area positioned some four stories in height above the intersection of Illinois and Washington Streets—is added to the new Mall setting, it is safe to say that the Circle Center Mall will have an enormous influence upon the national image of Indianapolis, Indiana!

Those fellows who traveled by train to our city several decades ago should somehow be able to see the changes which have been effected in that railroad area of our downtown. They would also be likely to share some disappointments among themselves over the disappearance of Pop June's Oyster House and the Mutual Burlesque Theatre. The Mutual was air-cooled decades ago by simply leaving the back doors of the theatre open during performances for better air circulation. This allowed for truthful built-in advertising of the theatre featuring "air cooled extravanganzes." But time did pass, and along with it the Mutual, and the Fox Theatre too.

Second story covered walk-ways will connect all of the new and existing buildings and parking facilities upon completion of the Mall and provide access to the greatly enlarged Convention Center at all times of the year. As an added, recently settled, new addition to the area will be a 13,000 seat open-air baseball stadium. The new baseball park will be erected just west of our famed enclosed Hoosier Dome, which seats 65,000 and is the home of the Indianapolis Colts professional football team. The Hoosier Dome, created a decade ago, is wisely connected to a Convention Center which has recently been expanded into a 300,000 square foot facility, one of the five best and biggest in the nation.

The Canterbury Hotel will have proud new companions in the downtown. Today at this four-star, four diamond hotel, we have an outstanding management team. They are led by an experienced lady named Tiki Moscrip, who has assembled a support team second to none of which I am aware. Vickie Jackson, another experienced and capable lady who managed the Downtown Hilton (now the Ramada Plaza) and Tiki were both trained as hoteliers by my admired friend Bob Meyer of the Airport Hilton. Passage of time will see female hotel general managers become ever more involved and prominent. We must remember that most ladies know home-related budgets and have an innate ability to allocate resources a lot better than many of their male counterparts.

Fred C. Tucker, Jr.

Before leaving "Development Efforts, Trials, Tribulations and Results" let me briefly mention our experience with Indianapolis' Union Station. Our team captain was the lively, imaginative, smart and enthusiastic Bob Beckmann—and we set out in the late 1970s to save this venerable landmark from demolition.

Indianapolis Union Station, a fine example of Romanesque Revival Architecture in this country was built in 1888 on the site of the first Union Railway Station in the world. (That first small wooden structure, later torn down for having been outgrown, was erected in 1853.)

Moving forward through many decades, our Union Station was the hub of downtown Indianapolis activity. It was from there that most of us went off to colleges and universities or met relatives and friends at holiday and festive times. More dramatically, during World War II the terminal saw most of us servicemen make arrivals or departures during those early and middle years of the 1940s. All of us often talk of overnight train rides starting off to school in various directions when we were thrilled to eat and sleep in a moving Pullman car enroute to our various destinations. Overnight then to New York, Washington, or elsewhere was indeed quite a contrast to our current-day air travel. To meet and talk to anyone these days who traveled by passenger train is to hear regrets that the comfort, style and convenience of train travel is disappearing from our daily lives.

In the early 1970s a local developer without extensive experience offered to buy the Indianapolis Union Station with a plan to demolish it and replace it with a high-rise office and apartment development. Mayor Lugar, sensing the historic value of this fine edifice, blocked the sale by the owner, the Indianapolis Union Railway Company, and talked our city council into buying the property. The mayor's plan was to hold the title to the building only temporarily, thus thwarting its demolition. He then immediately looked for private developers capable of purchasing the property from the city and doing a complete renovation of it.

Three different entities put in bids. One of these groups the Tucker Company created for such study and purpose, and the Tucker group was selected in that year of 1973. We presented an interesting team in our bid, composed of such leaders as Jack Baker, head of

Baker, McHenry and Welch, mechanical contractors; Dick DeMars of Geupel DeMars, general contractors; and the Tucker Company personnel, headed by the imaginative Bob Beckmann, all as proposed general partners of the entity bidding. To that group we added some twenty-five limited partners to our group known as Union Station Associates with such well regarded civic leaders as Gene Hibbs, Edna Lacy, Jim Browning, Roll McLaughlin, Phil and Jim Hedback, Joe Marmon and other Lilly executives all of whom also believed in "saving Union Station." We raised a half million dollars, bought it, stabilized it with a new roof, new gutters and complete outside cleaning and created a design to change the building's interior to retail, restaurant, and office usages.

About this time (1973-74) the Arab oil embargo set in, and inflation and interest rates started ascending. Such speculative projects throughout America became loaded with uncertainties. Our various bid prices continued to escalate and it soon became evident that without heavy public subsidies, our project could not be completed economically. Back we went to the city and with some federal funds assistance given in order to keep the building as a train and transportation center, we sold the Union Station back to the city, took a resulting financial loss to our group even after the historic tax credits then available, and went back to the sidelines, knowing that at least we had played a major part, although temporary, in "Saving the Union Station." The city then repeated the process of looking for new bidders. By 1978-79 Sandra and Bob Borns of successful apartment and development fame bought the building from the city. This dynamic pair created a dramatic Union Station show-case center at great expense, featuring all that all of us had hoped to see during that decade. The Borns later sold the finished product at no doubt quite some loss. To their everlasting credit, they saw it through and created a world-renowned, exciting center of activity for local people and visitors galore. Today the Balcor Company of Chicago owns and operates the finished product and, despite some recent problems, attendance figures are again on the rise. Those of us who are enthusiastic backers are thus predicting an ongoing success after a difficult road now covering twenty years for the venerable refurbished landmark.

A final thought about the fun side of such projects! During outside cleaning of the building during our watch over ownership events, we arranged for appropriate publicity to show that progress was taking place. Enthusiastic, lively Edna Lacy, one of the investors in the project and by then in her seventies, climbed up a step ladder with brush in hand to take her turn at exterior building cleaning. It was a windy day, and as she wielded her brush with her typical enthusiasm, up went her dress to a point where Dick DeMars, always a gentleman, stepped forward, lowered the garment and gallantly helped Edna back down the ladder. That was one incident which we should have photographed. Additional national recounting and publicity would no doubt have occurred, showing just what all has to be done to "Save a Station"!

Tucker Talk

In computing costs in real estate development, the more zeros there are to the left of the period in U.S. dollars, the higher the risk and less the likelihood of early liquidity! Translation: There is no room for ulcers and certainly no room for a non-entrepreneurial spirit!

PERSONAL AND CIVIC INVOLVEMENTS

"Don't join just to go to the meetings. If you don't believe you can make a difference make room for someone
who can!"

Anon.

To recount my own civic, professional and club involvements
would not only make one wonder if I ever had time to earn a living,
but might even read like horn-blowing by the writer. Let me dispel
both thoughts at the outset by saying firstly that I've never been on
welfare and secondly I neither need or want the recognition. Enough
of that has been my good but unsolicited fortune already. But let my
experiences, similar to those of others in my generation, serve as an
example to the less involved younger set of what one can *get out* of
civic involvement.

I suppose it all started with the Jaycees, where we learned, as
has already been said, "to learn civic service through constructive
action." This well-honed belief coupled with my deep feeling for my
community and for my profession have caused me to be more than
just an average participant.

First, let's discuss service activities within my profession. I am
proud that I have been one of eight in the Tucker Company who
have served as president of the Indianapolis Real Estate Board. Starting with my dad in 1944 and then with me in 1961, other members
of the firm including Bob Houk (1963), John Wallace (1968), Joe
Boleman (1974), Bob Fackler (1980), John Lewis (1984) and Bill
Grossman (1985) have also taken their respective turns at bat. And
now Ermajean and I are proud that Fred III is the president-elect and
will take over that assignment in 1995, making, I believe, the only
third generation person from the same family to serve the local Board
as its president. Our Board was founded in 1912, and now has a beautiful and functional headquarters building at 1912 North Meridian
Street (the site of one of our first Holiday Inns recounted heretofore).
Mary Binford, an effervescent middle-aged widow, served as the

Board's executive officer and became a legend in that capacity, well known throughout the entire country. She made everyone feel that any given great project was his or her idea, made every president feel important while she quietly corrected our mistakes, and most important of all was a true and supportive friend of every member. She "presided" when we hardly knew she was doing so, and when it came time for ladies to join the Board, she made it happen without incident, although in those earlier days it was a rather heated subject for debate.

One funny incident during one of our open debates on the subject at the weekly Board luncheon involved the then president of the board asking Marion Stump, a comic in his own right, why he, Marion, opposed women joining the Board. Marion quite uncharacteristically paused for a moment and then said "I'll be damned if I know!"—to the cheers of the supporters, who soon prevailed. Women have certainly made their marks in elevating the residential business to a noteworthy standing. Most of them involved are "meant to be" and are highly and professionally qualified as well.

I soon became involved with the National Institute of Real Estate Brokers, the largest of the nine Institutes, Societies and Councils of the National Association of Realtors (NAR) in those days and was elected to the presidency of that group in 1966. We met concurently but separately with the other NAR groups three times per year at various locations throughout the nation and headquartered with all at NAR headquarters in Chicago. Some of my closest real estate friends in America became so during those Brokers' Institute days and many of us have managed to stay in close and helpful touch ever since.

Chronologically I became the Indianapolis Realtor of the Year, the president of the Indiana Association of Realtors, Indiana Realtor of the Year and then finally president of the National Association of Realtors, the first person ever elected to that post from the state of Indiana. NAR still remains the largest business association in America, with over 800,000 members representing every state in the Union.

What a lasting and valuable experience Ermajean and I had in that assignment! We traveled over 150,000 miles, visited boards and associations in nearly every state, were inaugurated in Las Vegas and "sworn out" in Honolulu. During May of that year, we attended and participated in the International meetings in London, but had to leave early to return to Indianapolis for the famed 500-Mile festivities, including the nationally televised Parade and the Queen's Ball. Why? Because I was then also the president of the 500 Festival Associates. Obviously, we had to be present, but also we wanted to be there! Incidentally and many times over I have learned the value and importance of the chief executive officers of each organization of which I've become a part or have served, as either president or chairman. They are the ones - bless them all who cover up our mistakes, who provide continuity, and who know all of the answers to the handling needs of every crisis. Let me recount them in no particular order: Mary Binford (mentioned before) (Indianapolis Board of Realtors), Ferril Ressinger (Indiana Association of Realtors and permanent natural-born comic!), Jack Pontius (NAR CEO during my term of presidency), Dick Fague (United Way), Elmer Hill (YMCA during my term of office), Carl Dortch (Indianapolis Chamber of Commerce), John Walls (Indiana State Chamber of Commerce of which I was a director), Dick Rosser (President of DePauw University while I served as Chairman of its Board of Trustees) and Hugh Baker (Indiana Academy of which I am currently a trustee and regent).

Some of the most interesting ventures I immersed myself in in the sixties, seventies and eighties were not primarily for the company. They were public service efforts, and I did them because I thought them worthwhile, and because it was intriguing to be a part of the city's growth.

Let's switch to the Indianapolis Chamber of Commerce, over which I presided as president during 1974 and 1975, with the quiet but proud knowledge that I am, to my knowledge, the only person in Indianapolis to have ever served as both Junior Chamber and Indianapolis Chamber president. This was a gratifying experience because it carried out the continued commitment I felt to my beloved city from my earliest days in the business world. Carl Dortch, who succeeded the legendary Bill Book as executive vice president of the Indianapolis Chamber of Commerce, was a past master at making the elected head believe he was running the show. I've often told Carl that when anyone sought answers to a community need, I'd always say "call Carl," and the matter would be resolved. He and I worked closely together and have remained staunch friends. I have to add that when Carl retired, to his everlasting credit, he retired! It's a real talent for a person to get out of the way when he should, and we all see too many cases of those who are through, don't know it, and continue, provoking consternation on the parts of those succeeding them.

Tucker Talk

Get out of the way gracefully when the appropriate time comes and keep your advice thereafter to yourself. It will neither be understood nor appreciated.

I've mentioned the 500 Festival Associates, a dynamic group of civic-minded leaders who have fun with our famed 500-Mile Race and who help tremendously and unselfishly with our city's national image. Jo Hauck and her husband Kenny have made a great duet in leading the Festival, providing management and inspiration, and building the month of May to gigantic proportions for all involved both locally and nationally.

As already related, Ermajean and I flew back from the International Federation meetings in London for the 500 Festival Festivities. This gala included the magnificent parade in which we rode in a hansom-buggie, horse drawn, and the 500 Festival Formal Ball at the Convention Center. I had already told Jo Hauck, Executive Director of the Festival, some months before that I shouldn't assume the presidency of the 500 Festival that year because of the obvious time and place conflicts I was certain to encounter. But, as I've often said, "just leave the driving to the director." Jo carried out the assignments needed as though I had planned each one of them personally. I think it was not even noticeable that I was "in absentia in London" during the first few days of the May galas which surround the Festival and the city in annual excitement. Ermajean and I were on national TV during that parade, in all of our Gay Nineties regalia. We took a good deal of friendly ribbing from real estate friends throughout the country after that.

A word about the Ball that year. The 500 Festival Queen, chosen carefully by an impartial group of out-of-town judges, was this year a lovely brunette senior and Theta from Purdue with whom we maintained some contact in later years. It is customary for the 500 Festival president each year to start the dancing at the Ball with the Queen. Alas, as lovely as she was, she stood about a head taller than I—and what to do? The matter was settled quickly, however, "at ringside" by my suggesting to a handsome young law school student named Dan Quayle that he cut in on me shortly after we started dancing, and he did. Dan's dad, Jim Quayle, and I have been good friends for years since student days at DePauw, and Dan and our Fred Tucker III were classmates at both DePauw and Indiana University Law School. Marilyn, who is named Tucker but is no relation, grew up around the corner from our home at 54th and Delaware (she at 5300 Pennsylvania) and has been a friend of our daughter Lucinda from grade school and high school on. Any fellow who would so graciously "bail me out" on the dance floor with TV cameras whizzing, deserved my full support in later years, and he got it! When he first ran as an Indiana Congressman for the U.S. Senate, I was his first campaign finance chairman. My good friend, the late Tom Moses, CEO of the Indianapolis Water Company, quietly called the shots and raised the large monies in the background. Little did we know what would transpire in a few years to come!

Tucker Talk

If you have a tall dancing partner, don't hesitate to employ the services of someone taller than yourself. Perhaps all sorts of unexpected and interesting things will happen later!

Fred C. Tucker, Jr.

My work in the United Way, culminating in the job of president in 1976, came about by "going through the chairs" in the customary way. I was again aided and abetted by a great executive officer, one beloved by the whole community, the late Dick Fague. The campaign goal that year was $11,000,000. We raised it with a last minute push, thanks to the typical generosity of the corporate and individual citizens of Indianapolis. The goal each year these days approximates three times the amount Dick and I struggled to achieve. I take my hat off annually to each successive president who tackles the job so successfully. Regrettably, we don't have the generous home-based corporate ownership in Indianapolis that we used to have, and thus the charity fundraising job gets more difficult as time goes by.

An incident about United Way recalls that year of my presidency. Ermajean and I went downtown on the evening of the campaign kickoff on Monument Circle, amidst much excitement and fanfare. This hoopla included the lighting of the torch and the introduction of the United Way Child of the Year, representing the types of assistance rendered where badly needed through United Way support.

Any event of this nature has fanfare publicity in advance, so it was clearly evident that we were not at home that evening. I remember that Kurt Mahrdt followed us home after the ceremony with some papers for me to sign. Lo and behold, when we entered the backdoor, the three of us heard people leaving the house hurriedly, from the door leading out from the center hallway. Silverware was on the dining room table and on the floor, things were in disarray and when we reached the living room we saw that the front window had been smashed, originally allowing whoever had just left in a hurry to enter. Obviously our timing was fortunate, and of course the authorities soon arrived. They were, however, never able to catch the culprits, despite their best efforts. We were shaken, but we were lucky.

Let's recall now the Metropolitan YMCA of Greater Indianapolis which I headed as president for two successive terms. Our YMCA in Indianapolis was founded on Monument Circle over 125 years ago and has been a vibrant force for good since. Again I was made to "look good" by a great executive officer named Elmer Hill, recently deceased at eighty-one. Elmer was a career YMCA leader and was, indeed, one of the four or five best in the nation.

I "learned the ropes" at the feet of such titans as Earl Schmidt, co-owner with Bruce McConnell (Bob's dad) of the Hamilton-Harris Company, and Charley Saville, who headed the Sears operation in Indianapolis in those days. We built an exciting Family-Y system in Indianapolis and eight surrounding counties, which became a model for the nation. We added a summer camp, raised money, recruited great and supportive family members and had as many early-morning planning breakfasts as anyone could possibly attend, it seemed then, for a lifetime. Rapid growth geographically called upon our ingenuities, for when you add members at a tremendously rapid pace you must soon provide swimming pools, gymnasiums, and family programs in keeping with your promise to do so.

I will always remember a visit to see my friend through many years—Harold Ransburg, founder of the Ransburg Company—a tremendously generous person. After only ten minutes or so had elapsed in his office, Harold called his secretary in and told her to draft a letter for his signature, pledging a quarter of a million dollars to the Eastside Family YMCA, with the provision it be named after his father, Harper J. Ransburg. It still operates successfully under that name today. He did similarly generous things in those days too for Junior Achievement, Indiana Central (now University of Indianapolis) College, United Way and DePauw University. Harold died recently, obviously leaving a noteworthy mark on the needs of our city.

What about DePauw University, which I refer to so often in these pages? I suppose it is understandable that it is prominently featured, because starting with my mother and father our family has had sixteen people go through that university and receive wonderful educations. All of us are Methodists and are aware of the Methodist Church influences which have been so fundamental in the Green-castle institution through all the years. In fact, the presiding Methodist bishop in our area is by custom and constitution an automatic member of our Board of Trustees at DePauw. All of the bishops during my time have been active and strong supporters of the school.

Dad was a trustee of the university for several years before his death, so I suppose it was natural that I assumed a similar role in later years. As a result, I am now a life trustee, after having served on the

Fred C. Tucker, Jr.

DePauw Board of Trustees for some twenty years, including three successive years as chairman of the Board of Trustees of the University. It was during that time that a search committee was found to find a president to succeed Dr. William Kerstetter, who was retiring. Dr. Kerstetter had served faithfully and well as president during the early 1970s, when student uprisings and other crises on U. S. college campuses created over six hundred college president vacancies simultaneously in the United States.

Our search committee was ably headed by Dick Wood, then Chairman and CEO of Eli Lilly & Company and a strong trustee of DePauw. We met and worked arduously on locating a competent head for some fourteen months, interviewing applicants and searching out prospects. Everyone on the committee took assignments and made personal visits to the campuses and/or companies where our prospects resided. Curiously enough, one of my visits took me to Knox College in Galesburg, Illinois, where I went to see Dr. Lewis Salter. Lew was a distinguished science professor and a wonderful gentleman who wasn't an applicant, but who had come highly recommended from many sources. He politely indicated that he wouldn't become a candidate, but a few years later, of all things, he became president of Wabash College, where he served with high distinction for several years prior to his recent death. The keen and usually friendly traditional DePauw-Wabash rivalry is legendary, of course!

One weekend during that search period I went to Jackson, Michigan, to give the address representing our national college fraternity, Delta Tau Delta, at the centennial observance of the founding of the Delt chapter at Albion College. During the reception hour preceding the banquet that evening, I was introduced to the Albion dean, Dr. Richard Rosser, who, after our short get-acquainted chat, learned from me that I was on the DePauw presidential search committee. He called his lovely wife, Donna, over, introduced us to each other and then startled me by saying, "I am one of your candidates!"

Dick Rosser, who impressed me mightily that evening and certainly has ever since, came down to Indianapolis a few weeks later for the scheduled interview before the committee and was unamiously selected as DePauw's seventeenth President. He announced early in his administration that, in his opinion, no college president should serve longer than ten consecutive years, and true to his conviction, after a distinguished and highly productive career as DePauw president, Dr. Rosser retired. The Rossers moved to Washington, D. C., where Dick has just completed several years as president of the Independent Colleges of America, a post for which he was most admirably suited. He and Donna became good friends of Ermajean's and mine, and recent word from them indicates that they have returned to Traverse City, Michigan, where he can pursue his love of sailing and where Donna can continue her love of painting. She is a distinguished artist and donated an oil presidential likeness of her husband to DePauw University some few years ago. Dr. Rosser was succeeded as DePauw's eighteenth president by Dr. Robert Bottoms. Bob Bottoms and lovely wife Gwen continue to add to DePauw's illustrious history as her current "first family."

I had left DePauw in 1940, winner of a basketball letter gained primarily by excessive time spent quietly on the varsity basketball bench during most of the close encounters which DePauw played and which in some cases I probably helped lose. Still, during later years, my Alma Mater honored me in 1976 with the Old Gold Goblet given for significant service and in 1985 with an honorary degree as a Doctor of Public Service.

My association with Delta Tau Delta goes back just as far as my association with the university. Dad became the first family member to join Delta Tau Delta fraternity, an organization founded in Bethany, West Virginia, in 1858 and now consisting of some 125 chapters in various leading college campuses throughout America. When several of us went back to Bethany College in 1983 for the 125th anniversary of the fraternity founding, I observed that perhaps the eight founding members of the organization all of those years ago must have made it happen because of reasons of geography. If you ever found your way to Bethany, West Virginia, you would know that once there in those days it must have been difficult if not impossible to leave! The rugged hills and almost impossible roads for horse and buggy to "traverse" cause me to simply surmise that "there they were" a small group with lofty aims and purposes. They created a literary society which would later become Delta Tau Delta!

Counting uncles and cousins of mine, I believe our family has produced seven more loyal Delts (besides myself) since Dad's initiation into the fraternity in 1905. These would include my maternal-side cousins, Bob Oliver of Winchester, Indiana, and his son, Bob Jr., both attorneys, Joe Green, son of Dad's sister Ethel, Larry Tucker, Sr. and Jr., and Fred Tucker III. I was initiated into the fraternity at the DePauw Delt Chapter in 1937, with my Dad present and applauding!

Mom and Dad taught the meaning and importance of loyalty by their own examples. Their loves for Alpha Chi Omega sorority and Delta Tau Delta fraternity knew no bounds. As indicated before, they had to accept sister Emma Gene and me in Alpha Chi and Delta Tau Delta at DePauw because our dad would only pay bills there (and also, presumably because we proved acceptable to each organization).

Before going into the Navy I made a few chapter visits for the Delt central office headquartered in Indianapolis, including trips to the University of Iowa, Albion College in Michigan, and Toronto University in Canada. After the war, I would attend Delt functions with family members and friends and soon started through the leadership chairs of the national fraternity, which activity led to my becoming national president from 1974 to 1976. My good and long-time friend, Al Sheriff, became the chief executive officer of the Delt fraternity during those days and was my mentor. Al was, indeed, another example of a staff leader doing most of the work with the various officers taking most of the undue credit. Al came from the "huge town" of Cadiz, Ohio, and graduated from Washington and Jefferson College in Pennsylvania and Western Reserve Law School in Cleveland. He was a lawyer and bank trust officer in Cleveland, Ohio, and had an excellent background for taking over the top post of the fraternity after the death of long-time leader and friend, the late Hugh Shields.

Al taught me the inner workings of the fraternity, making me realize the real importance of what a fraternity does to inculcate high standards of conduct for life after college or university graduation. There are, of course, problems in continuity in the local campus houses. Leadership at each chapter rises and falls almost without notice. The average college fraternity career, of course, covers only a four-year span and just about the time a good undergraduate leadership team is assembled in any one of those chapters, graduation takes place, that group is gone, and you hope like thunder that new talent has been training in the wings. Lack of continuity thus causes many administrative and operating headaches. Without active, qualified and interested alumni support at each chapter, chaos often ensues, bills go unpaid, the physical plant deteriorates and a lot of the immediate future for just such a chapter is left almost to chance.

But a strong four-to-six man field staff of outstanding, newly-graduated Delts comes on board annually to serve for a year or two and are directed into the field by the central office to visit each chapter at least once a year. This visiting team has the responsibility of analyzing strengths and weaknesses at each such visit and is charged with improving and bettering everything and every person they come in contact with during the visits. The fieldmen also round up alumni leadership in each setting, contact university or college leadership for a "score-card" reading on each of the Delt chapters, and do what they can to address and improve town or city relationships as well.

At Al Sheriff's imaginative insistence, I agreed to help form the Delt Educational Foundation and became its first president. Since that time and under the tremendous and loyal leadership of Dick Englehart, Delt from Indiana University and longtime friend, the fraternity and its loyal alumni have raised over six million dollars, the income from which goes to support various needs and programs of the fraternity.

Tucker Talk

In fund-raising for any lofty purpose, gather a team, select a goal, and name a leader with a proven track record who believes in the mission and is committed at all costs to see that it is a success!

While serving as the foundation's first chief executive officer, Al died an untimely death in his late fifties, depriving it of his continuing leadership in the formative years of the foundation's growth. He was succeeded by another long-time friend and loyal Delt leader, Gale Wilkerson, a graduate of Oklahoma State University and top official.

For twenty-five consecutive years, leaving with mandatory retirement from each, I served on the boards of directors of Indiana National Bank, Indiana National Corporation, Jefferson National Life Insurance Company, the Jefferson Corporation and the Somerset Group. These were wonderful and educational experiences giving me an insight into the demands placed upon public companies by their shareholders, all of whom are investors and thus part owners of such enterprises.

Indiana National Bank was founded in 1834 and until its sale in 1993 to the National Bank of Detroit was, of course, the oldest bank in Indiana. The history of its growth and stability made it a legendary institution in our state. While I was a board member of the bank and the corporation, great leadership was provided by a series of chief executive officers, all of whom I came to know and admire very much. In order they were William "Pat" Flynn, Wilson "Bill" Mothershead, J. Kurt Mahrdt, J. Fred Risk, Tom Binford and Tom Miller. Tom Binford served for but two years after Fred Risk resigned, and many would say that the Binford era, short as it was, came at a critical time in the bank's history. It was this era, during the late sixties, when real estate acquisitions over a fairly short period of time grossly affected the bank's liquidity, much to the consternation of a good many seasoned shareholders. Certain ones of these acquisitions, however, later proved to be sound, but the non-liquidity hallmark of real estate can and has often caused the undoing of a good many well-intentioned involvements. And, sad to say, too many of these involvements wind up at deep discounts in the hands of those who weren't there in the beginning.

The bank meetings occurred monthly, committee meetings more frequently. Camaraderie with fellow directors existed through the years, much to my educational benefit. Being a bank director in any community imposes a responsibility of consequence, but affords such a member many business lessons and opportunities of lasting value. Tom Miller, scion of a banking father, native of Corydon,

Indiana, a fervent Indiana University alumnus and the possessor of quick wit and humor, will soon retire from the position he now holds of chairman and CEO of NBD—Indiana, after thirty-four years in the banking world. He will be succeeded by the ebullient, highly qualified Andy Paine, beloved by all, graduate of DePauw, and an outstanding community leader in his own right.

Jefferson National Life Insurance Company and the Jefferson and Somerset Companies have been extremely well run and managed by the McKinney brothers, Kirk and Bob, who in my estimation have been two of the most outstanding and well qualified CEOs in our community. Their late dad, E. Kirk McKinney, Sr., was a good friend of my dad's and made a name for himself in both business and politics in Indiana. Kirk, the older of the two brothers and a University of Michigan graduate, ran Jefferson National Life. Until his recent retirement following the sale of the company to another publicly held life company in Texas, he was well recognized nationally as a life insurance leader. He remained for a few years on the board of the acquiring company, but he and his wife, Alice, bought a home on Puget Sound in the state of Washington. They go there with regularity; Kirk teaches as a visiting professor and lectures at colleges in that area.

Bob McKinney, a graduate of the Naval Academy and of Indiana University Law School, is heavily involved in business, academia, and politics. He served as Chairman of the Federal Home Loan Bank Board in President Carter's Administration in Washington, D. C., now heads First Indiana Bank (the principal subsidary of the Jefferson Corporation), and recently was named Chairman of the Board of Trustees of Indiana University. His record and his involvements at top levels speak for themselves, and he and his wife "Skip" are a couple of well-known, respected Indiana citizens.

Knowledge gained and contacts made with these directorships have proven invaluable as adjuncts to my own career, and I am grateful for the opportunity to have had these exposures through a period of over a quarter of a century. Eventually, of course, it is time to go. Some public companies, although very few, pay perhaps too little attention to retirement age requirements on their boards of directors, but I stand very strongly in the corner of those which mandate age seventy as "retirement time." Moving the older echelon out constantly brings along fresh blood and new ideas. The shareholders are entitled to just such rotations and after all, in my case at least, twenty-five years of service served as an appropriate span. I am proud that our son, Fred Tucker III, now serves on the Board of NBD - Indiana, and I can assure all that his election was *not* nepotism. He earned the position and qualified for it on his own.

Through the years, and as evidence of my diverse interests and involvements, were my receipt of the Indiana American Legion Distinguished Citizens Award, the Boy Scout Lifetime Eagle Scout Award and the March of Dimes Quality of Life Award.

Politics and its nuances have always been a favorite hobby of mine. Over thirty years ago the political arena could possibly have developed a different career for me but for the admonitions and advice of my wife and my parents, who were fearful that I was going to head in that direction.

In the early 1950s I served as chairman of the Alex Clark for Mayor Committee. In his mid thirties, Alex, a great guy, a longtime friend and an erstwhile suitor of my sister Emma Gene - became the city's youngest mayor in history. I didn't look for involvement after the election. In time, however, I became chairman of the Republican Veterans of our county and later of our state. Following that was a significant involvement in the successful campaign of Mr. George Craig for Governor of Indiana. George, a native of Brazil, Indiana, and a practicing lawyer there with his father, had had a distinguished war record. This record had helped catapult him into the highly visible office of National Commander of the American Legion. George was a masterful speaker and ran for Governor at age forty-two, concurrently with the Eisenhower for President national campaign. George won the governor's race handily and served effectively until some of the Legion friends who surrounded him after his election violated laws and principles, thus causing an unfortunate blot on George's term of office. George Craig was the typical trusting type who was misused by his friends. His budding political career for higher office was thus thrust into oblivion.

Being involved in two such victories for the mayor and governor allowed me to meet a good many Republican leaders in our area.

More than several of them would suggest from time to time that perhaps I should become a candidate myself. The climate and the settings of my age and my exposure were such that I believe with a lot of effort and help I could have obtained the Congressional nomination in our district. With the Republicans then dominant, I could then perhaps have a seat in Washington representing with others the state of Indiana and my constituency. But as I've said, wife and parents wisely prevailed, I backed off from such a potential path. If I had been successful, I would have suffered a probable loss of productive business years, not to mention potential financial problems or losses as a result. I've known of few, if any, elected figures in politics who have returned to private life better off financially or in other ways for having served.

Tucker Talk

The old and true one! "All that glitters is not gold!" And what a perfect example for anyone contemplating a political involvement!

One of the nicest, unsolicited things that ever happened to me was to be honored and named to the Junior Achievement Central Indiana Business Hall of Fame in its second year of its recent existence. This occurred as a pleasant surprise in 1990. My fellow honorees were Lou Jenn, investor, businessman, close friend and the founder of JennAir, and two deceased citizens. They were Madam C. J. Walker, the first African American woman to ever earn a million dollars from meager beginnings with a beauty supply business of national note and a famous Hoosier, the late Frank Sparks, entrepreneur, co-founder of what later became Arvin Industries, and later President of Wabash College. My whole family attended the recognition ceremony, which made the evening a sentimental success for me.

Bud presented a fifty-year Tucker service pin to his mother at the
company banquet in 1968 with Bob Johnston beaming his approval.

The Banner-Graphic

VOL. 5, NO. 193   PUTNAM COUNTY, INDIANA, WEDNESDAY, OCTOBER 9, 1974

Honored Saturday

Fred Tucker named top alumnus

Indianapolis businessman and civic leader Fred C. Tucker, Jr. will receive DePauw University's "Alumnus of the Year" award in ceremonies in Greencastle Saturday.

Presentation of the Old Gold Goblet for "eminence in life's work and service to Alma Mater" will be made by DePauw President Dr. William E. Kerstetter.

The ceremony at a 9:45 a.m. convocation in Gobin Church will be among the major events of Old Gold Day-homecoming activities at DePauw. this weekend. Keynoter for the convocation will be Dr. Henry Steele Commager, noted historian and scholar.

Tucker is a 1940 graduate of DePauw. He has been a member of the University's board of trustees since 1967, including the past five years as board vice chairman and a member of the committee on investments and athletics. Last year he assumed additional responsibilities as chairman of the steering committee of DePauw's Second Design for a Decade development program.

"Bud" Tucker is one of DePauw's distinguished graduates doing imaginative work through his profession in Indiana and throughout the nation," Dr. Kerstetter said. "At the same time, he is exercising important, creative leadership in the life of the University."

Tucker is president of the F.C. Tucker Company, Inc., Indiana's largest realty and development company. He serves as director of several other corporations and in 1967 was named Indiana Realtor of the Year.

In 1972, when he was serving as president of the National Association of Realtors, Tucker also served as a Presidential appointee on the U.S. Price Commission's Rent Advisory Board.

Tucker has served the city of Indianapolis as he has served DePauw. He has been president of the Chamber of Commerce, chairman of the YMCA Foundation, president of the Junior Chamber of Commerce, and president of the "500" Festival Associates of Indianapolis.

Recently he was elected president of the Delta Tau Delta national fraternity.

Tucker was selected for the Old Gold Goblet by vote of the directors of DePauw's national alumni association. The association's president, Andrew Paine, Indianapolis, will introduce Tucker Saturday.

Other DePauw alumni who have shared the Old Gold Goblet through the years include a Secretary of the Navy, a Secretary of the Interior, a former commissioner of baseball, chairman of the TVA and AEC, college and corporation presidents, and a retired commandant of the U.S. Marine Corps.

Fred C. Tucker

Children of Bud and Ermajean Tucker are: Lucinda, age 8; Fred III, age 10.

The grand opening of the Indianapolis Hilton was May, 1970.
Above (l-r) Barron and Marilyn Hilton; Erm and Bud Tucker were
happy attendees at the Hilton extravaganza.
Below (l-r) are Barron Hilton, Bud Tucker, and Conrad Hilton

(Top) Gary Warstler, first Tucker Senior Award winner was presented
at the Tucker Company kick-off banquet.

(Bottom) The Four Partners, mid 1970s, are
(l-r) John Wallace, Bob Houk, Bud Tucker, and Joe Boleman.

And in 1994 we still are, because we still do!

(Top) At our "Home Away From Home" in Admiralty Point, Naples, FL are ninety-nine units developed with others in 1975. We are on the seventh floor in the very middle.

(Bottom) A budding athlete was Fred Tucker III, age 10.

SALE OF THE TUCKER COMPANY

"There is a rare premium on good judgment!"
                                    Fred C. Tucker, Sr.

I sometimes reflect on that truism spoken often by my dad, not as a lecture, but as a statement. It continues to ring in my ears as being accurate.

By the early 1980s we had built a pretty sizable company and for various reasons and involvements had become well known nationally, as had our slogan "Talk To Tucker." It was, then, no particular surprise that we were contacted on several occasions by the Coldwell-Banker and the Merrill-Lynch companies, both wanting quite frankly to buy the Tucker Company with stock or cash or both. I took these offers into careful consideration. It had long been my own plan to provide for succession of leadership and ownership of our company. I also was determined to carry out a personal responsibility to see that John and Bob and Joe were handsomely rewarded for their years of loyalty and efforts for our company. Their gain would be mine too, as we were equal partners, but the challenge was to arrive at a time, place, and price. I was 67, Bob 65 and Joe and John 62 during that period. Bob by then had a fine son-in-law, David Goodrich, who had joined the firm. He and Fred III were fast becoming good business and personal friends. But my three great partners were not necessarily "ready" to sell, and I don't suppose I was either. We all did agree that we owed to our many fine associates (by then I suppose some eight hundred people and their families) a responsibility for continuity. After all, they had all been giving so much to the company's growth and each had a right to know what the future held. Obviously, if we sold to a public company, a new direction of methods and leadership would probably be introduced. As is often the case in such happenings, the "local people touch" could well be lost. In addition, since we had become the dominant leader in real estate in our area, it was logical to ask if perhaps in a merger or a sale with a public company, we wouldn't be bringing more strength to the table than they.

We talked to others whom we knew well nationally in real estate to seek judgment and advice. The Henry Miller Company of Dallas was, and is, perhaps the closest replica to the Tucker Company; Henry Miller and my dad had been close real estate friends preceeding my long friendship with Henry, Jr. He and I knew each other well through the National Institute of Real Estate Brokers and the Realtors' Washington Committee (the lobby arm of our national Realtor movement which I ultimately chaired). I made a few trips to Dallas to meet with Henry and even to see if there was any synergism between the two companies which might cause a friendly merger and ultimate national expansion.

Interestingly enough, the Miller Company was sold in a stock transaction to a public real estate company, Grubb and Ellis, based in Oakland, California, and we finally did decide to sell out to Fred III, David Goodrich and Jim Litten in January, 1986, for cash. Our three new partner-owners have continued to keep the Tucker Company quite forceful and have expanded it very successfully.

Let me describe individually Jim Litten, David Goodrich and Fred Tucker III, the present owners of the Tucker Company.

Affable, energetic and with the build of a football player, native Ohioan Jim Litten is a graduate of Ohio University at Athens, Ohio. He became a rising residential real estate star as co-manager of the Tucker Keystone at the Crossing Office some years ago. Jim worked under the tutelage of Joe Boleman and Gary Warstler and was their obvious choice to be the ultimate successor to lead the residential division. Married to Susan, a top flight residential sales leader in her own right, and the father of three attractive daughters, Jim became a certain choice to join with Fred III and David Goodrich as a new one-third owner of the Tucker Company.

David and Fred, as son-in-law and son of company owners, obviously were logical choices for the other equal thirds owners-to-be. Jim Litten, however, had no such family "roots," and because of that independence, he became a very important factor in the buy and sell negotiations which ensued. He could remain completely objective, and on more than one occasion helped to overcome hurdles which arose by encouraging the other two to not get unnecessarily bogged down in too many family concerns, no matter how well founded personally some of them were. They, of course, had to exercise extreme care because of family ties. They also had to be careful not to offend, push or delay, despite anxiety that the "big bite" they were about to take with heavily borrowed money might cause sleepless nights. On many occasions I did talk quietly with Jim to encourage him to make it happen, realizing that I could talk to him as a sincere friend who wasn't in the role of a relative. Jim Litten was an unprejudiced balance wheel in what we were trying to accomplish.

This is not to infer that David and Fred were being difficult, but it was obvious that they had to be extremely careful not to create a situation which, if it ultimately didn't work, would have serious repercussions in each family. And, of course, since most of the purchase had to be structured with borrowed money, the three buyers, Jim, David and Fred, took major risks in personally guaranteeing the repayment of the borrowed funds to close the deal. So it was with real relief and pride that I finally realized that the deal was complete. The company that my father had founded with such sacrifice and that so many of us had worked over forty years to develop into a respected state-wide force was now in good hands for the future.

David Goodrich, a native of Michigan, and graduate of the University of Michigan with an M.B.A. from the University of Virginia, came to the Tucker Company from the Continental Bank in Chicago some eight years prior to the sale and purchase of the Tucker Company. He is the husband of Marion's and Bob's daughter, Julie. Together the Goodriches make a great team, a driving force in Indianapolis. David is highly organized, a most pleasant and engaging individual, and has in his own capable manner become a community leader. Julie and David have two fine youngsters, a daughter, ten and a son, seven at this writing.

What else with some attempt at modesty can a dad say about a son which has not already been said? Fred III has been true-blue to the cause of continuity for the Tucker Company as a third generation president of that business. As a lawyer by training and experience, he is careful and analytical. A confirmed team player with Jim and David, he is quiet, thoughtful and good at analysis. Together the three of them have fashioned a remarkably effective partnership. They paid off their initial and sizable bank debt ahead of schedule. In addition, they have encouraged and effected growth of the company in terms of both people and real estate management. They've added ancillary businesses, including title insurance, parts of construction management, growth in insurance of all types, an auction affiliation, and the opening or joining of about a dozen offices through acquisition or franchise all over the state of Indiana in the Tucker Company affiliate name.

This new management team carries its respective roles with vigor and commitment. They're among the top fifteen or twenty such organizations in the United States. I guess what I am saying is that, happily, the risky arrangement is working. Had it not worked, it would well have been "Woe-Begone" for the four original interests created back in 1958!

Tucker Talk

Carefully planned succession in business ownership doesn't always bring effective results. However, right-meaning and right-intentioned people working on both sides to bring it about can eventually make it work! The Golden Rule—the Tucker Company credo—worked its marvelous way again!

With some risk, however, I feel motivated to make a critical observation about today's Tucker Company with some comments that won't be overly popular to some who read this. A few years ago the company became an owner-partner with some two dozen other such companies in the United States in an entity known as Collier International. This combine includes real estate companies throughout the world, and the obvious intent is to create and foster national and international real estate referral business amongst all such owner-partners, no matter what their comparative size and location. All of the companies, I am certain, are highly competent and qualified.

But the net result of this activity has created a "dual image" for the Tucker Company which is bound to be confusing to our long-established clientele, for years so instrumental in the Tucker Company growth. Indianapolis, by even a stretch of imagination, is *not* an international city of consequence. At least 95% to 98% of the Tucker Company business, volume and income, comes from both local and state primary and referral business. Perhaps, over 80% of the Company business has always come from and continues to come from its residential division. How else could it be, frankly, with such a heavy predominance of people and listings and sales in that division?

The highly effective advertising so long established and carried out by residential signage (Block "T"—"Talk to Tucker"—yellow and black colors), numbers of people, market dominance, and highly visible results have been the leading factors in the company's growth through now nearly thirty years. Yes, the growth and dominance of commercial - industrial and management divisions has also been truly remarkable, and continues to be so.

But the terminology of "Collier-Tucker" in advertising, telephone communication, and reporting gives the impression that either two companies now exist side by side or that another company has been created. And the different signage would surely imply that such is the case.

I may be wrong in my observations and recognize that my view could seem self-serving, narrow and egotistical. And if the volume of Collier-referred business to the Tucker company is more than I believe it to be, then I stand at least partially corrected. I have never been accused of being against a national and international presence for the Tucker Company (and have demonstrated that by my own personal real estate association involvements), but I have yet to feel that we fall as a city and as a company into the national and international arena of importance. We are just not that big nor that dominant.

And while I think of it, I should cite a comparison of referral business which works so well under Sandy Warstler's guidance in the

Fred C. Tucker, Jr.

field of national and local (and yes I'm sure international) referrals from one city and location to another. This operates under the same old thirty-year old Tucker sign, logo, and banner and brings additional dollars and results to the company's residential division.

My sincere tribute now has to go out, however, in the final analysis to George Charbonneau and David Goodrich for their commitment to and zeal for the Collier International Association. George has been a loyal Tucker Company member and leader for over thirty years and has distinguished himself markedly by recently serving as national president of the Society of Industrial and Office Realtors, one of the most distinctive honors that anyone can achieve. And this has brought a large amount of business, thanks to George, to the Tucker Company's non-residential doors.

George served for years as a most effective head of the company's commercial and industrial division. At the appropriate time, after being David's most effective mentor, he turned over those duties of leadership and organization to David Goodrich. What David has done to propel growth, leadership, and high visibility since has produced tremendous success. And David, like George, will also surely someday head one of the national real estate organizations because of his competence.

And so, back to "Square One." I hope my comments about potential confusions to the public prove wrong and that "all is well that continues well." It is my only violation of my commitment in 1986 "not to meddle," so please forgive this transgression for what I deem to be that important and significant. I have been there, and I admit that I always was a wary person!

As recent evidence of their community involvement, each of these three fine young men has distinguished himself and the Tucker Company as follows: Jim Litten as the new chairman of the Indiana Real Estate Commission, David Goodrich as new chairman of the Methodist Hospital Board of Directors, and Fred Tucker as president-elect of the Metropolitan Indianapolis Board of Realtors. You can bet that John Wallace, Bob Houk, the late Joe Boleman and I, who started into real estate so long ago in that small but happy office, are exceedingly proud of all of them!

BELIEFS, CREDOS, AND PREDICTIONS

This is where the author, the holder of the pen, sitting in an uncontested position can wax philosophical. These ideas which follow are my own and seem to come off the end of my pen as though they have been wanting to do so for a long time. Most of them aren't new, and I have referred to them often.

Advice for Business Success

- Obey The Golden Rule

Whatever better credo for any business or personal enterprise than that for almost any situation? "Do unto others as you would have them do unto you!" Unselfishness pays huge dividends and is always recognized for what it is.

- Don't be limited by The Third Generation Rule

It is often said that almost any enterprise cannot succeed in family succession for three consecutive generations. I have never believed this, because such a statement presumes factors that cannot be predicted. There is no reason why continued commitment to basic beliefs and principles in business can't survive ad infinitum. The Tucker Company, I believe, is fortunate to be an example of one such history which has worked, and principally because each of the Fred Tuckers has not been unwilling to give credit to others.

- Emphasize good surroundings

This doesn't just refer to physical surroundings, although we have always tried to provide excellent physical places for our people to gather and to work. We have always believed that such amenities speak well for us vis-a-vis the public. But what I mean by "surroundings" refers to people. It is a known axiom that he who surrounds himself with competent, bright, sympathic people will benefit immeasurably, particularly if he doesn't care who gets the credit for success.

- Pay civic rent for the space you occupy

This credo is a measure of what we all do to "pay back" the advantages afforded us by community, state and nation. Everyone needs to be a participant in the great effort to improve one's surroundings and to literally make the place better than the way one has found it. But to join and participate for only business reasons destroys the fun of helping out and eliminates the joy of giving. Serve for the sake of giving!

- Be slow to anger and quick to forgive

As we grow older we find too many occasions where difficulty appears to be the "other person's fault." Holding one's temper in difficult situations can often be a real challenge. If we are on the receiving end of unpleasantness or misunderstanding, it behooves each of us to be reflective. We need to analyze cause and effect and if possible be a healing and not a destructive force in trouble. How many times do we "wish we hadn't said it," and how many times do we remember how difficult it has been to apologize as a peacemaker or help the "offender" by saying "forget it" and mean it? No one is PURFICK!

- Know that you can make a difference

The lowliest and the newest recruit or the most seasoned veteran is always impelled by a need to make things better. I happen to believe that each of us is on the face of this great earth to help others and to literally make a difference in things and in situations near us. "Someone has to do it and it might as well be me" says one philosopher who believes, and rightly so, that waiting around for others to make a difference wastes opportunity. We need to make a difference! It brings real satisfaction to do so.

- Tackle the tough ones head-on

The most debilitating habit one can form is to avoid the unpleasant! The irony of such avoidance is that the problem will still persist in a festering state, and until a person tackles and tries to solve it, it won't go away! Set the lesser daily challenges aside for the moment and solve the vexing one first. Remember how much better and relieved one feels when he or she has "conquered and not succumbed"? So do it—now !

- Realize there is some good in everybody

Now come on, one may say, bank robbers, rapists, murderers, and the like? Well the best authority we have is the Bible and the saving doctrine of the forgiveness of sins. But on a lesser level, where no felony is involved, we have a bounden duty to find the best in our fellow beings and not be critical of their habits. We hope that they are thinking the same about us!

- Avoid the complainer

Better yet, try to change the perennial griper's outlook and behavior by a practice of "Yes—But." We can raise the negative person's consiousness by offering an opposite view after first "understanding" the complaint or criticism. Constructive listening can often dissipate the unpleasantries of a frustrated person.

- Know that "The more the zeros left of the period in U. S. Dollars the more difficult the transaction is to complete."

Now here is one for study and understanding. It is not to say that the smaller the real estate or other transaction the easier it is to complete, for each one invariably has its hurdles to overcome. But from personal experience I can attest that any transaction dealing with U. S. Dollars in at least seven figures is bound to be fraught with near-endless hurdles and delays, all enough to test the proverbial patience of Job! The type of business in which we are engaged teaches patience, fortitude, and indeed the ability to understand complicated matters.

- Understand that mistakes can't be undone but they needn't be repeated

Through all of the years we operated the divisions of our company on a rather autonomous basis. As I've attempted to relate heretofore we did make mistakes, a lot of them. But as partners we took responsibility for any mistake any one of us made, vowed not to repeat it, and encouraged the saddened one to forget past errors and go on as if the mistake had never occurred. It was always great for all of us to have the comfort of partnership and friendship, and to this day

I am forever grateful. We didn't make many, but some of the mistakes we made, in reflection, were "doozies"!

- Don't ever lose your sense of humor

And if you lack that, you must work hard to develop one. Often a humorous note interjected into a trying and difficult circumstance can make a marked difference in the outcome. We know full well the value and the fun of being with someone who adds a note of genuine levity to a situation, and according to some experts the well balanced individual invariably has a sense of humor as one of his or her main attributes.

- Be optimistic

The optimist is one who more often than not is the winner. This isn't to say that all optimism is well founded. Still, on balance, intelligent optimism based upon prevailing facts will often keep a dialogue alive until solutions to difficult problems are found. And besides, just who dotes on being around a confirmed pessimist?

Fred C. Tucker, Jr.

PREDICTIONS

Without an infallible crystal ball it is nevertheless fun and invigorating after some fifty years in the business to "look into the future" with respect to the practice of real estate.

I believe . . .

• Private ownership of residential housing will continue in this nation as the cornerstone of individual security and worth. There will, however, be increasing attempts to turn home ownership into a public utility with prices and sizes and amenities being controlled by the public sector. Such attempts will be masterfully defeated by the associated strengths of groups like the National Association of Realtors and the National Homebuilders Association, ably supported by all segments of our national banking and credit systems.

• More innovative stylings of our residential dwellings will occur throughout the nation. With more families led by two breadwinners, ease of running and maintaining a home will become simpler, with additional "push buttom" aids to bring such changes about.

• More innovative financing to help and assist the first-time home buyer to enter the market and changes in our onerous national tax system will favor the home owner in America more than ever before.

• The real estate industry will become the most visible and prevalent force in America for leading our nation's people back to the belief in and practice of family values. The family which works and progresses together, which owns and lives in a home together, will again become America's most vital force. The attempts to down-grade or demean the family will prove more and more unpopular. This doesn't necessarily foretell a "return to the good old days" (whatever that may mean) but it does predict that the family will be as impor-tant in the future as it was at the turn of the last century, before great advances in transportation and communication in the 20th Century brought about more fluidity in family life.

• The real estate business, to be successful, will demand in-creased education and professionalism for all of its practitioners. Women will continue in ever increasing numbers to dominate the residential brokerage arm of the business. They are, as I've often said, the ones who know where the grand piano and the davenport go - and they have the innate ability to create an imaginary scene for the lady-homebuyer. They are, in addition, capable business people on their own, as they are demonstrating in our company. And, the old adage that the ladies buy the homes and men pay for them still stands in many cases, even in this two-income world.

• The U.S. tax code greatly affects the practice of real estate, particularly in the non-residential areas of expertise. Predictably, and because of pressures upon national leaders from clear thinking citi-zens, we will see reductions in the capital gains tax. We will experi-ence a return to a system of incentives calculated to again bring the American entrepreneur back into the marketplace, thereby creating renewed employment and job opportunities.

• The Tucker Company will continue to grow, prosper and re-main dominant so long as the Golden Rule prevails and a sense of family and cohesiveness continues to prevail among its leaders and their associates. All know full well that it is "harder to stay there than it is to get there!"

Fred C. Tucker, Jr.

Tucker Talk

Emerson's Essay on "Compensation" holds that in the systems of life there are correlative happenings which tend to exert long-lasting and dominant influence on the future. His essay says in effect that in life every dark has a light, every hot a cold and every night a day! This says that those in positions of dominance cannot take that dominance lightly and must always be wary of change and of uncontrollable happenings. As an aside along this line, I think back to a wood carving which I bought in Stockholm, Sweden, showing a bare tree branch reaching to the sky with one little elf with a broad and satisfied smile perched at its top. He is shown as looking out and up, but unfortunately he fails to see two small elves climbing up the tree branch looking toward him, both with determination on their faces. And to complete the picture so cleverly carved on this limb, two more elves stand at the base of the tree looking up with countenances indicating that they fully intend to climb the same tree and replace all three of the elves above them. I have used this elf "prop" many times when I give talks about the challenges of competition and complacency. It is clearly worth noting in the real estate business.

Optimistically speaking, however, the futures for both the practice of private real estate and for the Tucker Company appear very bright to this writer.

PARTNERS, PEOPLE AND FAMILY SUPPORT

My three business partners, John, Bob and Joe, have already been described elsewhere but are all deserving of further mention. Because of their complete unselfishness in often burying their own remarkable identities for the good of the cause, the F. C. Tucker Company is what it is today! I marvel at how we were thrown together at young ages with the avowed purpose of succeeding together. I often recall how, in our early days we would live the adage that "misery loves company." No matter how difficult business times might become, at least one of us would make a sale or a lease with a fee sufficient to feed all of us. And we all ate, played, worked and survived together as we grew, professionally, in our business. Credit in spades must be given to Sarah Wallace, Marion Houk, Martha Boleman and Ermajean Tucker. Different though they are, each has basic traits of loyalty and perserverence—just what we needed at various points in our growing careers. I suppose it is fair and accurate to say that while we worked and learned and grew they raised the total of eleven youngsters among them and kept the home fires burning!

Elsewhere I have talked about my own family background. Perhaps inadvertently through emphasizing Dad's influence, I may have not given full credit to the influence of my great mom. With all due and proper respect for influences on my life from two grandmothers, a mother, a wife, and a daughter, I doubt that I have ever known a more remarkable lady than Mom.

Mom was in the truest sense a lady of letters! She was very well educated, articulate, highly refined, loyal, a motivator, a Bible student of note, a teacher of Latin and English, and a collector of aphorisms. She inspired our youngsters, taught them about nature and the heavens, took them for long walks in the woods, all the time teaching about leaves, and trees and birds, and the firmament and its importance. She inspired them like all of us to help others, to work and succeed, to be modest and yet forthright in our opinions, and to have a genuine concern for others. At eighty-five years of age Mom wrote a small book entitled "Yesterday." This remarkable testament includes vignettes of her childhood, her own family, her days at DePauw, her marriage to my dad, and her absolute delight in her children. Mom made us understand many common things and mysteries, made us believe in ourselves, made us appreciate the smaller and important things, such as her devotion to her parents, and her love of being a wife and a mother.

April Fool's Day was my annual target for special notice of Mom, and I made every effort to fool her with some silly prank like "Did you get my message in the mailbox?" (no message there) or "did you forget to call so-and-so?" (no such call needed). She pretended I had fooled her into doing something inane or foolish. Each year on her own birthday, July 6th, she always gave my sister and me a present (as we were giving her gifts) saying that she wanted to show her appreciation for her own children on her birthday because of the joy she felt they brought to her. "Tis more blessed to give than to receive" —and Mom lived that Biblical advice in so many fine ways.

And now a brief word or two about my maternal grandfather, Judge Frederick Sidney Caldwell (from whence I got my two given names). A brilliant lawyer and jurist and an Indiana Appellate Court Judge, he was above medium height and build and had a strong shock of white rather thick hair protruding a bit over his ears in today's somewhat mode style. He was known for his quiet wit and humor, which, when employed, made for unforgettable stories around our family circle. As youngsters, we called him "Dade," and he was always glad to see us and interested in what my cousin, Bob Oliver, and my sister, Emma Gene, and I were doing.

He owned and drove one of the first Haynes automobiles manufactured in Kokomo, Indiana, and was notorious for being one of the world's worst drivers, always hugging the middle of every road rather than remaining in his own lane. Two stories of humor and "road-position" will illustrate. Once while heading west on the Old National Road (now U.S. 40) from Richmond towards Indianapolis, a driver heading east managed to stop "Dade" before nearly being crowded into an adjacent ditch. They fell into a brief conversation and the fellow then asked just how far Dade would guess it was to Indianapolis. My grandfather, according to his passenger that day replied: "Sir, in the direction you are heading it is approximately 25,000 miles!"

Partners, People, and Family Support

Another story demonstrating his middle of the road driving tells of another fellow coming towards him, slowing down (cars still didn't move very fast in the early teens) and shouting to my grandfather in a loud voice: "Jesus Christ, lay over!" Dade's passenger reported back that the only retort the complaining fellow received was: "Sir, I am afraid you have identified the wrong party!" Dade lived to seventy-eight and was greatly saddened and made lonesome by the loss of my lovely, quiet grandmother, Emma Stewart Caldwell, who preceded him in death by some twenty years. My two grandmothers were named "Emma," which of course accounts for my sister's first name.

My mother died in late January, 1979, at the age of ninety-one. She had enjoyed excellent health until the last year or so during which time we were able to keep her in her home, with full-time attention, in accordance with her wishes.

We were a closely knit family and appreciated each other— and as I think back on it we all brought different personalities to the situation. Dad, serious and yet fun and outgoing, and a "people" person, a sentimentalist and a loyal friend; Mom, bright, responsive and yet more reflective; a balance wheel and one who often preferred small gatherings or just staying at home away from the din and noise; sister Emma Gene, bright, witty, life of the party, artistic, sensitive, and possessed of a million friends; and Bud, perhaps a literal composite of the traits of all three of them, Dad, Mom and Sister, and the one best able to get by with the most because of being the youngest!

Compared to a good many families we never had an abundance of relatives. The ones we did have were and are unforgettable and have been additional influences on my life. Mom had wonderful parents, each of whom came from somewhat larger families, and her youthful days in Winchester, Indiana, a county seat of about 10,000, were a positive influence on her later life. She had a younger sister, Gladys, who unfortunately died at forty-nine. Today's antibiotics could have saved her. Gladys and her husband, Harry Oliver, had one son, Bob, who later went to DePauw, Indiana University Law School, and then practiced as a highly successful lawyer in Winchester. He died at sixty-nine and his son, Bob, Jr., one of Bob's and Jane's five youngsters, followed in his dad's educational and legal footsteps and now based in Winchester is the Randolph County, Indiana Prosecutor. He and wife Beverly (they met at DePauw) have one daughter and Bob Sr.'s widow, Jane, a lovely lady, resides in Winchester with all of the youngsters and grandchildren close by. Dad's older sister, Ethel, and her former husband, Frank Green, lived in Normal, Illinois. They didn't enjoy the happiness and success to which they were entitled. Five youngsters, all of whom scattered with their own interests and careers, did provide Aunt Ethel solace and comfort from a failed marriage which had left her in fairly desperate straits. Her two brothers, Dad and Larry looked after her in later years. Ethel is buried in Hume, Illinois, where the three siblings were born.

My uncle Larry was articulate and outgoing, a true personality. He never really got into the "swing of business." He married well however (the saying today is that "he was on a full scholarship!") He and his first wife, Mildred Carpenter (from a wealthy Cincinnati family) had two youngsters, my first cousins, Susan and Larry, Jr. and lived together as a family in Detroit and Bloomfield Hills, Michigan. Mildred died in an automobile accident. My cousin Susan, a lively, attractive, and accomplished young lady, married Hjalmer (Luke) Rindal of Neenah, Wisconsin. After becoming the mother of Stephen (since deceased), Susan died in childbirth with daughter Susan surviving. Susan Rindal, just now turned forty, is the "spitting" image of her mother. She resides in Atlantic Beach, Florida, adjacent to Jacksonville, filling her life with pep and humor and interests in horses and autos.

Uncle Larry later married a widow, Ethel Olson, whom he met in Indianapolis, and until his death at age eighty-three lived with her and Larry, Jr. and Larry's wife in southern California. Ethel, again a widow and a lovely lady, now resides at Leisure World in California. She has just reached the tender age of ninety-nine!

As to my own immediate family, they remain affectionate, helpful and loyal to "Bud," the husband and Dad! Ermajean, my best friend and strongest supporter, is as pretty and as much fun now as she was fifty years ago when we first met in Los Angeles during the war. When I first met her dad in that hurried war time, he said, "She will never let you down." She hasn't! Ermajean deserves the lion's share of the credit for the two fine youngsters we have! She has earned more true friends than anyone I have ever known. A boatload of birthday cards arrives every year from far and wide, full of endearing messages. Ermajean is the epitome of the truism, often repeated by both our mothers "To have a friend you must be a friend."

Ermajean's older sister, Norine, was divorced from Bob Isgrigg. The mother of three fine sons all of whom have wives and families of their own in Pontiac, Michigan, Norine has proven herself the nicest, kindest sister-in-law any fellow could have.

To go back a generation, Ermajean's and Norine's devoted parents were John Angus and Erma MacDonald. Their mother, who came to the Pontiac area from her native Vancouver, Canada married their older dad at age eighteen. Their dad died at age seventy-eight and then their mom, little in stature but mighty in courage and pep, died at ninety-one in January, 1993. That was exactly the age which my mom had attained at the time of her death just eight years earlier to the month.

Fred III is a pretty good example of a Man for All Seasons. He is taller and larger than I and, I suspect smarter. Fred's a lawyer by training and for awhile practiced that profession. A good husband, dad, and golfer, he has a host of friends, and is the third generation successor president of the Tucker Company, as was emphasized earlier.

Fred met Becky Morris of Tipton, Indiana, only child of Kathleen and Chet Morris, a retired mortician, at DePauw and they graduated there together as classmates in June, 1969. They were married the following October in the Methodist Church in Tipton. Incidentally, that's the night I quit smoking for good on a fifty dollar bet with the Morris' family physician. Luckily, he and I were both too tight to lose the bet! Fred Tucker IV (who will finally change the family's first name?) is a talented guy, 6'1", 180 pounds and I think handsome as can be. He is a sophomore at the University of Virginia, which he chose on his own thereby breaking the family habit of "where does one go to college?" He is an excellent student, interested in nature, geography, biology, the universe, and comparative religions. Fred is a triathalon competitor, and in the summer of 1993, he went to San Antonio as a budding prospect for trying out as a penthalon athlete (swimming, fencing, running, bicycling and horseback riding and jumping) for possible entry in the 1996 Olympics. His future is surely bright.

Fred C. Tucker, Jr.

Bright and beautiful with dark hair and eyes (Grandfather talking) his younger sister Betsy surrounds herself with interesting, attractive people with similar interests and backgrounds. She is a junior at Brewster Academy in Wolfeboro, New Hampshire, making friends wherever she goes. Clothes and style conscious, she could well become a model, but whatever she does she will do well. She's filled with pride and a "want to do well" attitude.

Their mother, Becky, is a talented artist who put a potential career on the shelf to raise those two youngsters and who has devoted countless hours to effectively fulfilling that assignment. No two children have ever received more love with more unselfish advantages given them.

Our cute and highly capable daughter Lucinda Ann is literally one of a kind. She has the Tucker and MacDonald trait of being a friend. Her A.B. degree and Masters Degree in Education are from DePauw. Her additional Masters' Degree in Career Guidance and Counseling is from Indiana University, where she served as a counselor for some six years after teaching English in Danville, Indiana, and being a business owner in Greencastle. Chris Maron, her first husband and her classmate at DePauw, is a Greek Adonis in appearance. He was center on the football team and is a "nice guy" from Tarzana, California. They graduated in 1971, were married a couple of years later, and lo and behold after a "friendly divorce" (whatever that means) Lucinda married Bob Kirk of Columbus, Ohio. Bob, best man at Lucinda's and Chris' wedding, had never married. Now how's that for excitement? Lucinda and Chris have one daughter, Carmen.

Bob Kirk, also of the class of 1971 at DePauw, serves as English teacher and track coach at Columbus Academy, a venerated private institution of K through 12, which has just "gone coeducational" some three years ago. Bob makes an ideal member of the family of three and serves as surrogate father to Carmen, who's now a full-fledged successful, and popular student at Columbus Academy in Ohio's capital city. They have recently bought a larger home in Bexley (part of Columbus) and Lucinda now teaches Freshman English at Ohio State University. Carmen (please excuse Grandpa) is also headed for something great and again carries out the family trait of friendships, solid and many. She is very attractive, studious, athletic, and tall like her dad. Carmen has a wonderful manner and disposition and will always be a happy person surrounded by talented and interesting people. She is indeed a leader!

Tucker Talk

Never underestimate the importance and value of family heritage, practice, and commitment, for this is the element in society which perpetuates the best in all of us!

Almost as close as family is Sally Carbaugh, who served as my administrative assistant in business for twenty-five consecutive years! Possessed of keen intellect and of an even and cheerful disposition as one might ever see, Sally has been a tower of loyal strength to me and a helpful ally to each member of my family through all of the years. Every friend and business associate of mine "knows Sally" and all recognize that she has been at the core of most of our victories and has helped in defeats. When I have said as I introduce her, that "Sally is the only one who really knows what's going on around here" it has been more often true than not. Sally comes from Stamford, Connecticut, and Springfield, Ohio, as an only child. She entered Shortridge High School as a sophomore upon her parents' move to Indianapolis and graduated from my old high school. She has two married daughters and seven grandchildren. Sally prefers sun and water to snow and ice and in retirement will predictably be found in such surroundings. She deserves the highest praise that both I and the Tucker Company can give her. Sally retired in the Spring of 1994 and was succeeded by Brenda Jackson, a friend and ally of the Tucker Company through the years and one who has many of the same characteristics as Sally.

Some years ago, when our office headquarters were still in the Indiana Bank Tower, I had some three dozen 8 x 10 photos, arranged alphabetically, mounted on the south wall of my office, and once a year, at Christmastime I invited this group to my office for a bit of Christmas Cheer in order to say thank you to each. Those singled out are people who have made significant contributions to the Tucker

Company and to my own career in so many unselfish and meaningful ways. Of course, all of them couldn't be there annually, but their photos served as a daily reminder to me of what they have meant to me as I said silent words of appreciation to each.

Beyond family so many have helped along the way. Let me mention a few. I served as best man at three different weddings during the early days. The last of the three was for a friend from childhood, James Carter, who married lovely Leah Porter while he was in the Army and I in the Navy, in the Los Angeles area. James, now deceased, was the son of our family physician, mentioned in the first chapter. Dr. Carter was the one who chased me at age six through the house, caught up with me, and vaccinated me while holding me down under the dining room table. I guess I remember that pretty well every time I see a medical needle heading my way. Dr. Carter used to say that if he had to select another career, he would go into the hardware business, because the hardware products (spades, shovels, saws, etc.) never change in style and they are needed for every household in America. I wonder what this patient, bright, and humorous family friend would think today of the strong push for socialized medicine. This ominous threat keeps inching forward in a country where private ways of doing things have until now been the order of the day.

Jean Knauss and Bill Welch, both of Logansport, Indiana, were married forty-five years ago in Jean's family home. The nuptials took place on a March Saturday afternoon at 4:30 P.M. That wedding was small. Jean's sister, Virginia, was matron of honor, and I served as best man. Ermajean was "very much" in attendance, since our daughter Lucinda was born just six weeks later! I always told Ermajean that she "stood out" more than anyone at that wedding. Bill, my college room-mate and close friend for now over fifty years, after naval service in the Pacific and graduation from Michigan Law School became an eminent and highly successful lawyer in Indianapolis. Steady, bright, articulate and fun, he never changes, no matter the day or the hour, representing that one person outside of family in a lifetime who will always stand by a friend when needed, on a moment's notice. He and Jean have a son Brian and daughter Sarah, and four bright grandchildren born, two each, to those two and their fine spouses.

In another war time wedding, summer of '41, Dewey Lindley and Bob Morgan were married in Danville, Illinois, at her family church. I became best man when "Skin" Maxwell, by then already an Army pilot, couldn't be there for the ceremony. Dewey was the daughter of Judge and Mrs. Walter Lindley, he of the U. S. Seventh District Appellate Court. The senior Lindleys were always a fine and thoughtful hostess and host when the Welches and the Tuckers would join Dewey and Bob in Danville after Illinois football games.

The Lindley-Morgan wedding itself took place on a Saturday afternoon and went off *almost* without a hitch. I drove Bob to the church in an open Ford convertible, resplendent in a white jacket, and just as he was ready to enter the sanctuary of a church with friends and relatives, we spotted a smudge of grease (from that darned convertible?) on his right shoulder. The minister, obviously one who had responded to many a crisis in his day, almost as if by magic produced a bottle of white shoe polish, which we applied to the spot. Presto, the wedding proceeded on schedule, with me hoping that no other happening might arise to mar such a beautiful occasion.

Dewey and Bob have now been married some fifty-three years and have remained, with the Welches, our closest friends. They have also been blessed with one son and one daughter, and to date they have won the Grandchildren Derby among the six of us with a total of six, compared to our three and the Welches four. Bob Morgan graduated from Harvard Law School, was an Army pilot instructor during the War, and practiced law in a superb fashion in Indianapolis for over forty years until his fairly recent retirement. He and his firm employed Fred Tucker III as a young attorney for some four years before Fred joined the Tucker Company.

Marvin Hackman succeeded Bob as our company lawyer and has been of inestimable help to everyone in our company since. Not only is this kind, considerate Jasper, Indiana, native one of the best real estate lawyers in Indiana, but he is a good and close friend upon whom I rely for answers when needed in business, banking, and sometimes even in golf! He and lovely wife Jane have raised four outstanding youngsters, three sons, two of whom are attorneys and one who is in sports administration, and a physician daughter specializing in infant cardiology.

Where would I go from there to name and describe so many others who have been important to the company and to me? Bill Armstrong, Bob Johnston, John Wood, J. D. Sawyer, Phil Smaby, Chuck Ryan, Jack Ryan, Al Fernandes, Jim Wagner, Dave Easlick, Reed Bartlett, Bill Elder, Jack Neff, J. B. White, Joe Dowd, Charlie VanTassel, John Stewart, David Wilcox, John Myrland, George Charbonneau, Tucker Hawkins, Gary Lewis, Steve Burkhardt, Bif Ward, Peggy and Paul O'Kane, Gale Wilkerson, Ken File, Keith Steiner, Lu and Wes Martin, Dick DeMars, Boris Meditch, Dave Queisser, Dave Jessee, Wayne Timberman, Barney Hollett, John Tucker, Wade Neal, Hiram Rogers, Bart Grabow, Tom King, Tom Miller, Andy Paine, Nick Frenzel, Jack Hare, John Holliday, Harry Meyers, Bob Fackler, Bob Orr, Andy Phillips, Eddie Craft, Buck Bradley, Tom Brady, Sam Davis, Bill McMurtrie, Jeff Madtson, Bob McConnell, Bob Netherton, George Vyverberg, Tom Binford, Pink Persons, and West Shell are only part of the list.

There is one special group I need to single out. Over thirty years ago I spotted a four night/five day ad in a golf magazine featuring Pinehurst, North Carolina, a spectacular golfing mecca which ranks alongside St. Andrews, Scotland, and Augusta National in Georgia. Our first foursome to Pinehurst was made up of Bill Stout, Don Fobes, Stewart Ruch and me, and the following year we added Alex Carroll, Bob Morgan, Gene Hibbs and the late, great Dr. Ricks Madtson, who by all odds was our most ardent golf enthusiast—and that is saying a rather large mouthful!

For twenty-nine consecutive Octobers this eightsome went to Pinehurst without a change of personnel, until we lost our great buddy and outstanding surgeon, Ricks Madtson, to an untimely death at age sixty-eight. Dr. Ricks was a Kansan from Ottawa, took his medical training at Kansas Medical School and grew to be a noted Indianapolis surgeon, beloved by all who knew him. When we used to play thirty-six holes a day on the earlier outings, we would worry a bit about playing that much golf at once. Ricks would always say, "I'll be the sole arbiter of when we will restrict ourselves to eighteen holes per day." He was replaced by Boris Meditch, whose game and demeanor added lustre to the group. We took turns being tour chairman, always played four days, stayed at the Pinehurst Hotel or its well appointed cottages and just played golf until time to go home. Each spring the chairman (by rotation) would schedule the group for trips to other well known golfing spots. We covered places like Las Vegas, Pebble Beach, Myrtle Beach, Sea Island, French Lick, Hilton Head and Naples, Florida, just to name a few. Alex always arranged the pairings and Stew always ran the pari-mutuel betting, consisting of $2.00 bets in various combinations. They claim that I lost the trophy between trips, but it wasn't so! I know beyond question what happened to it, but that information is privileged and not to be revealed. Twenty-nine years seemed to spell "adios" for the regular outings when Gene Hibbs died, but nothing could ever diminish our fond regard and deep friendship for one another and our appreciation for a life-long experience and camaraderie with the close friends who have made up the Pinehurst Group!

A word about Gene. Gene Hibbs started his own business of the manufacture of corregated boxes in 1946, built it into a highly successful enterprise and sold it to a nationally rated company in the late eighties. He probably won the trophy annually more often than any in our group, an accomplishment for a golfer who was self-taught through both practice and acquired knowledge. Gene's wife of fifty years, Nancy, with whom I went all through high school, proved to be the official photographer of the Pinehurst Group through all of the years and compiled a book from photos of each gathering with the wives which occurred after each one of the annual outings. Gene died at eighty in 1992 and as mentioned earlier was a longtime, close, Delt fraternity friend of mine. He is missed, as is Ricks, very much.

After executive positions with Pitman-Moore, Allied Chemical and Armour and Company in the chemical business, Stewart Ruch bought the National Printing Plate Company in Indianapolis and built it into a very successful company holding many patents and with an international flavor. He and I graduated from high school together and he went on to Butler and then to Purdue for his degree in pharmacy. He lost his dear wife, Jane, to polio a few years ago and has since been happily married to lovely Ann Kixmiller, widow of Bruce and good friend of ours, of Naples, Florida. They now divide their time between Naples and Indianapolis. He and his son, Bill, now president of National Printing Plate, and son Fred III and I plan a trip to Scotland for ten days of golf intermingled with the last two days of the British Open.

The greatest "by ear" piano player of all time retired at age fifty-eight as head of Paper Package Company, an Eli Lilly subsidiary. He just turned eighty-two, and often shoots his age on the golf course! Even-dispositioned Don Fobes and his truly genuine, lovely wife Shiela have been close friends through all of the years. Unlike many other talented pianists, Don will sit down and entertain all present without urging. An amusing and interesting Wabash graduate is Don Fobes.

Bill Stout and vivacious and pretty wife Harriet move about from time to time and certainly escape monotony while providing moving occupation for others. Homes at 4000 N. Pennsylvania, followed by 8100 College Avenue, a move to Arden, a condominium on Mystic Bay, two condominiums on Florida's East Coast, another in Naples, Florida, and now most recently a move to the Jacksonville area qualify them as a real estate broker's dream! Bill has had an outstanding double career, first as Executive Vice President of L. S. Ayres & Company and then as Development Director of Wabash College. His easy transition from one post to another and his strongly developed loyalty to Wabash, felt even though he is an I. U. graduate, makes him most unique.

Boris and Marian Meditch are classmates—graduates of Northwestern University and are both great community and civic leaders. As a matter of fact four of our group—Hibbs, Carroll, Meditch and Yours Truly — have all served as Chairmen of the Indianapolis Chamber of Commerce, thereby showing that we have done other things than play golf. The Meditches, like all of the original group, have been good and loyal, caring friends of ours through all of the years.

Alex Carroll, native of Indianapolis and our "all American boy," is married to lovely Marilyn, a native of the San Francisco Bay area. Alex is a noted stockbroker and is nationally known as one of the originators of investment clubs which were so prevalent some years ago throughout the nation. He has been our chief game arranger and scorer, performing his services without flaw. Alex is a graduate of Williams College and the son of a former president of Indiana Bell

Telephone Company.

Bob Morgan completes our "august group" and has been chronicled elsewhere in this book. Since he and wife Dewey moved to Florida after his retirement from the practice of law, he probably has made the most distinct change of any of us. A fine fellow who used to operate quietly and effectively in the background, Brother Morgan has now become the consummate political type who knows everyone, speaks to all and provides more funny stories than all of us put together. To see his fine game of golf being exercised almost daily with groups of people who look forward to his entertaining and relaxed status, you would never know that he has endured not one but two open-heart operations. Most of us believe that he is the best example of the "perfect retiree." He can be found daily at the Royal Poinciana Golf Club in Naples, Florida, in the winter and at the Meridian Hills Country Club in Indianapolis in the summer.

As I have said earlier, the national headquarters of Delta Tau Delta sent field men annually around to various campuses. They were in our city in the summertime and thus all got acquainted with our family. Mom and Dad would have them at our home for Sunday dinner, Dad would arrange golf games for them with him and me at Hillcrest Country Club, where he belonged and which he had helped develop, and we all became fast and loyal friends. To this day my own friendships with them have endured. Gene Hibbs, now deceased, was a graduate of the University of Kansas. John Fisher from the University of Tennessee, Ken Penfold from the University of Colorado, and Bud Murphy from Penn State became in time my own embodiment of the Four Horsemen of Delta Tau Delta! Gene founded Dura-Containers, John Fisher became Chairman and CEO of Ball Brothers Corporation, Ken Penfold, after serving as alumni director of the Colorado University, became a prominent Colorado Realtor. Bud Murphy recently completed a highly successful career with the Westinghouse Corporation. I have remained close to them and they with me for over fifty years.

Travel has played an important part in our lives, too. Ermajean and I through the years have traveled extensively, and by actual count have visited some twenty-eight countries around the world. It all started after my own Navy experience with Uncle Sam's courtesy visit to the Pacific, followed by a 1955 experience with Radio Free Europe which took me to Munich, Germany, Paris, France, and Berlin, Germany. After that Ermajean joined me and we traveled then through Germany to Switzerland, Italy, France and England. We came back to New York flat broke, after six weeks aboard the SS United States. Emma Gene and Bob met our two smiling faces.

Nearly twenty years later, Dick DeMars and I took a trip to Dhahran, Saudi Arabia, hoping to become involved in medium-rise apartment development in that area. Our contact was the project leader on our Admiralty Point venture in Naples, Florida. One Chip Hutchison had been sent there upon completion of our project to start just such ventures.

Dick and I flew to London, then to Beruit. After landing only briefly, we went on into Dhahran, Saudi Arabia, where we met brother-in-law Bob Hall. Bob and Emma Gene were then living in Hong Kong. The three of us had several meetings with Chip Hutchinson and Saudi principals, and upon our return Dick attempted to involve Turner Construction of New York in our proposed venture. Our efforts were full-fold, our trip was very interesting, but time and distance negated results.

A couple of years later Ermajean and I made the same trip into Saudi Arabia, spent time with Chip Hutchison and his wife again in Dhahran, and then flew to Jeddah by way of Riyadh, the capital of Saudi Arabia. Our trip then took us to Cairo, then to Geneva, and finally back to the United States. The experience of seeing Saudi Arabia came freshly to mind a year or so ago, during the skirmish which took place in that area during the last year of the Bush administration. Earlier, we took a YMCA trip with others to Sweden, Hungary, Romania and Austria, and a DePauw-sponsored trip to Norway, Poland, Russia and Finland. We have made three or four trips to Hong Kong, Bangkok, Manila, Singapore and briefly into China, all for fun and educational experiences. Some ten years ago we took our youngsters, their spouses and our grandchildren to England aboard the Queen Elizabeth. It broke down in the North Sea for three days. Our entourage headed west from England to Paris, back to London, and then we returned as a group on the Concorde. What a wonderful family experience.

We have gone with other couples on planned golf trips through-out Scotland and Ireland. Fred III and I did a Father-Son one with others throughout Scotland, playing again some of those great courses. With the Realtors we have been to Alaska twice, travelled many times to Hawaii, and also covered parts of New Zealand and Austra-lia. And now that the Wall has fallen and the Iron Curtain has dropped, I'm hoping visits to Poland and Czechoslovakia are in the not-too-distant future.

Tucker Talk

Take advantage of travel opportunities and broaden your horizons. The world was meant to visit and the human mind and intellect are intended to grow through extended contacts.

There is a significant omission in this story. Perhaps I have saved it for last because of its importance. I haven't covered "Church" an important facet in every "believer's" life! Mom was a member of the Christian Church, where her lawyer dad taught Sunday School for probably fifty years. Dad was raised by a devout Methodist mother; DePauw is a Methodist-related university. Ermajean was raised as an Episcopalian, although her father at one time was Catholic. Methodism, though, won out eventually in all of our lives (or took over). Mom and Dad were pillars in the Meridian Street Methodist Church where Mom, like her dad, taught Sunday School for years. My sister and brother-in-law were married at the old Methodist church at St. Clair and Meridian Streets. Dad acquired the ground and helped to build our present United Methodist Church at 55th and Meridian Streets. Ermajean became Methodist with me and our two youngsters were baptized at our present church. We could be better "attenders," but all of us are believers. I have been a member of our church since infancy. We now have the sixth pastor there during my own lifetime, certainly all outstanding leaders. Logan Hall married my sister, Dick Lancaster buried my sister, and Bill Schwein,

Fred C. Tucker, Jr.

DePauw graduate, now serves as our senior minister. Interspersed among these were such leaders as Virgil Rohrer, Abram Woodard, and Frank Templin. Our church, always a meaningful presence in the community, has had a long and successful history.

On a personal note, I try to say my own prayers in private solitude and on bended knees each day. I *do* know from many, many personal experiences that there is a Being and do know with complete confidence that we are guided by a Force stronger than any of us Who sees to our wants, knows of our sins and our troubles and stays beside us through all needs forever. It couldn't be possible with all of our human experiences and our relatively short lives that a Hereafter doesn't exist for us all, where we again will see our forebearers and carry on with some masterful meaningful direction. To pray is to believe, and to see wonders and results brings untold comforts to those in need and desirous of help.

PHOTO ALBUM

This chronicle would not be complete without sharing with you some of the people and events that have been so important in my life.

Space does not permit me to include all that I would like. The photos on the following pages have been culled from hundreds. They are of necessity, incomplete. But how do you choose from such a rich and treasured collection?

The best I am able to do is to pick those that highlight key events and influences in my life. Family and friends, of course, have been the obvious choice with a sprinkling of those special associations that are so closely entwined in the *Tucker Talks* story.

Each photo in the album has a special place in my heart and life. It is my pleasure to share them with you.

(Top) President Reagan is shown with Realtor friends in the mid 80s at Washington, DC. (l-r) Bud Tucker, Indianapolis., David Jones and John Wood, Naples, FL.

(Bottom) Running for the U.S. Senate, Dan Quayle and his Finance Chairman, Bud Tucker, in 1984.

Thirteen Tucker Professionals! (on a mission) [l-r] Jack Gambs, John Jewett, Joe Schaub, Wayne Timberman, Kurt Mahrdt, Percy Kleinops, Dave Jessee, Jim Schrage, Bill Moore, Mike Walker, Mo Thomas, Bob Houk, and George Charbonneau. (early 1980s)

Two lovely grand-daughters (early 1980s) are:
Carmen Maron and Betsy Tucker.

On a trip to Washington, DC are (l-r) JackWilliamson (Realtor's
Washington Committee), Bud Tucker (Chairman, RWC), Erm Tucker
with President Gerald R. Ford (1980).

Tucker Company Sales Contest winners in the early 1980s are
enroute to Europe! None look any older today!

In St. Andrews, Scotland, in the late 1980s "At the Old Course" are (l-r) Harry Meyers, Judge Jack Ryan, Adele Rice, Joanie Elder, Erm Tucker, Bud Tucker, and Bill Elder. Lady Mike Ryan, non-golfer is not pictured.

Original Pinehurst group (l-r) Hibbs, Ruch, Carroll, Stout, Tucker, Madtson, Morgan, Fobes. Mid 1970s.

Bud receives the Honorary Doctorate degree at DePauw University in 1985.

TUCKER TALK

F.C. TUCKER COMPANY, INC.   VOL. 8 NO. 8   DECEMBER, 1987

TUCKER GOING STATEWIDE

Charlie Ashby

Those in attendance at the All Company Meeting held October 14 at the Airport Hilton heard it firsthand: the Tucker Company has created a statewide brokerage and management network to be known as F.C. Tucker Affiliates, Inc. At the helm will be **Charles C. Ashby,** a well known and respected Realtor from Evansville.

In making the announcement, **Fred C. Tucker, III,** president of F.C. Tucker Company, Inc. said, "Creation of F.C. Tucker Affiliates, Inc. is designed to extend the services of the Tucker Company into broad areas of the state. It will help us be more effective marketers of real estate and provide access to buyers and sellers we might not otherwise reach."

Fred went on to say that discussions on both potential acquisitions and franchised affiliates are underway with several realty firms around the state.

Charlie Ashby, immediate past president of the Indiana Association of REALTORS, commented, "By offering Tucker services, Tucker name recognition and the Tucker reputation as one of the oldest, biggest and best real estate organizations in Indiana since 1918, we can help our affiliates increase both sales volume and profitability. It is our hope that Tucker and its affiliates statewide will be selling approximately 10% of all homes on the market," he stated.

F.C. Tucker/Huber Realtors

School for Thought

The Real Estate Career & Development Center, a real estate school offering sales and broker courses statewide, has been established as a private venture by the three principal owners of the Tucker Company. Messrs. **Litten, Goodrich** and **Tucker, III** have formed the LGT Corp., a privately held corporation which will operate the school. Chosen to serve as the Center's director of education is **Betty McConkey,** an experienced teacher of real ·state courses and the former owner of her ⌄wn real estate firm. Two types of courses will be offered by the school: the Sales course is designed to teach the fundamentals in preparation for the state exam (as well as the fundamentals of the day-to-day

real estate transactions through instructor experience); the Broker course is designed to teach and assist the sales person in understanding management needs (budgeting, recruiting, office organization, philosophy, advertising and more). These courses will be offered in three curriculums: four-week accelerated daytime salesperson classes, eight-week salesperson evening classes and eight-week broker evening classes. The cost to Tucker sales associates and personnel is $175.00; cost to non-Tucker persons is $250.00. Classes are being held in Indianapolis, Evansville and South Bend. For more information, you can call 639-0519.

Betty McConkey

After the start of F. C. Tucker Affiliates and new real estate school in 1987, the enterprises expanded state-wide in some ten other communities.

Just talk to Tucker

INPLS NEWS
11-27-93

When folks say "Talk to Tucker," there's a good chance Tucker will be around to listen. This year marks F.C. Tucker Co.'s 75th year of service as a leading real estate management and brokerage firm in Indiana.

Percentage points are always important in real estate, and Tucker can claim another percentage of distinction: Its longevity is equalled by less than 1 percent of all real estate firms in the nation.

Tucker started out in 1918 as a one-person operation run by Fred C. Tucker Sr. The reins were passed to his son, Fred C. "Bud" Tucker Jr., in 1957 and remained under the latter's control until he was bought out by his son, Fred C. Tucker III, and two other partners in 1986. Currently, the firm employs more than 1,000 staff and sales associates in Central Indiana and key cities statewide. Annual sales exceed $1 billion.

Tucker is the largest independently owned real estate firm in Indiana. It ranks as the 28th largest independent residential broker and the fifth largest independent commercial broker in the United States.

Co-owners Fred Tucker III, David Goodrich and James Litten anticipate healthy expansion in the years ahead. The trio plans to enter more Indiana communities and possibly even branch out to neighboring states.

Best wishes for F.C. Tucker's continuation as a significant employer and real estate service provider in Central Indiana.

(l-r) Mess'rs Goodrich, Tucker and Litten

Bud and Fred Tucker IV are shown in San Antonio in the summer of 1993 at the Olympic tryouts for the pentathalon by Fred IV.

Erm and Bud enjoyed the 500 Race in May, 1994.

My 1992 Christmas Card. (Bud and friends) was a
"Thank you for your support!"

Still in Charge? Bud's Christmas card December 1993.

Tucker Thoughts . . .

What follows are bits and pieces of information that may be of interest to you—either for trivia purposes or so that you may better understand our community.

At the most recent meeting of the Corporate Community Council, I was briefed on two major sports changes in Indianapolis. First, you may know that Indianapolis will no longer host the U.S. Clay Court Tournament, but do you know why? The Men's Professional Tennis Tour has organized itself into play on three types of surfaces, namely clay, grass and hard surface. The three major tournaments representing each surface are the French Open, Wimbledon and the U.S. Open, respectively. The top professional tennis players are committed to competing in tournaments that offer comparable surfaces leading up to the three major events. Thus, the only way to continue with clay court play in Indianapolis—and to attract quality players—was to play in the early spring leading up to the French Open. Given our ever-changing weather in the spring, outdoor play was questionable at best. Thus our local organizers elected to position the Indianapolis tournament as a tune up to the hard court U.S. Open Championships. The courts currently are being converted to hard surfaces for a tournament which will take place during the first week of August, 1988. This first week in August date will be permanent with the Men's Circuit, and negotiations to attract the Women's Circuit are under way. The rest of the long range strategy calls for the maintenance of at least four clay courts plus the addition of grass and permanent indoor courts so that Indianapolis can become a major training center for young, aspiring tennis juniors, who need to train on all types of surfaces.

One of the better kept secrets in Indianapolis is the construction of a facility (behind the Natatorium on the IUPUI campus) to house the National Institute for Fitness and Sports (NIFS). This facility and its director (Bud Getchell, PhD) and his staff will strengthen our claim to being the Amateur Sports Capital of the World. The mission of NIFS will be to focus on the development and disbursement of knowledge that will enhance the fitness of all Americans. Research, teaching and testing will be offered to all—from the most skilled athletes to individuals interested in improving the physical fitness portion of their life styles. Nearly 51% of our illnesses are caused by our life styles, and 25% of our illnesses are caused by our environment. The key to reducing these percentages is to exercise. NIFS will develop a four-step process that will help all interested in developing appropriate exercises to enhance one's life style. The steps include (1) awareness, (2) assessment, (3) creation of a personal exercise/nutritional program and (4) the support expertise needed to train an individual to maintain nutrition and exercise programs on his/her own. Keep your eyes and ears open for future information about NIFS—not only will it enhance Indianapolis' image (and thus attract more business and people to the city)—but it can also be of assistance to each of us personally as we strive for greater physical fitness.

Finally, want to see how you stack up with the average American? Well, a recent survey noted the following traits of the average American:

1. Reads at least two books per year.
2. Laughs at least 15 times a day.
3. Has 4.6 cavities.
4. Eats 92 hot dogs per year.
5. Is sick 6.5 days per year.
6. 61% believe in "love at first sight."
7. 64% of adults wear glasses (see 6 above).
8. Six in ten exercise daily.
9. "Damn" is one of the 15 most frequently used words.
10. 66% feel that they are young for their age.

We were in Singapore at the Goodwood Park Hotel for Erm's 70th (with Chairman of Support Group) July 1991.

WALL OF THANKS

The photos shown here, in no particular order, are several of many who have made individual and significant contributions to my growth and career. Each one of them knows of such contribution and so do I, but this gives me a chance to recognize several who helped to make up this Wall of Thanks. Would that space would permit the showing of so many more.

Frederick S. Caldwell

Fred C. Tucker, Sr.

Fred C. Tucker, III

Roy G. Altman

William S. Armstrong

E. Joseph Boleman

John Burkhart

Alex Carroll

Danny Danielson

Richard B. DeMars   Carl R. Dortch   John W. Fisher

Donald B. Fobes   Marvin L. Hackman   Robert Hall

Eugene B. Hibbs   Robert E. Houk   John R. Jewett

Robert A. Johnston   Richard L. Lancaster   John A. MacDonald

J. Kurt Mahrdt, Sr.   Boris E. Meditch   Robert D. Morgan

Kenneth C. Penfold   H. Jackson Pontius   Eugene S. Pulliam

William E. Rife

J. Fred Risk

Richard F. Rosser

Stewart E. Ruch

J. D. Sawyer

Alfred P. Sheriff, III

William J. Stout

John A. Wallace

Gary B. Warstler

Ben J. Weaver   William F. Welch   John R. Wood

Our Recent Family Photo

1st row, (l-r) Carmen Maron, Ermajean and Fred C. Tucker, Jr., Fred C. Tucker IV;
2nd row (l-r) Lucinda Kirk, Robert Kirk, Fred C. Tucker, III, Becky Tucker, Betsy Tucker.

EPILOGUE

"The hardest work is to do nothing!"

Anon.

A book on any subject needs to have an underlying purpose to make it both readable and perhaps usable. This one has been "brewing" in my mind for many months. Let me describe what I wanted to do with this effort and why it took so long in an embryo stage to finally bring it into being.

My initial purpose and thought was to create a motivational book which might inspire younger people entering or growing up in today's business world. Knowing that with proper applicaton, a zeal to succeed, and the ability to visualize the road ahead, things do happen, I wanted to share some of my experiences and personal philosophy with others.

I thought initially that if I, and others in our company, were to tell the story to a third party I could direct the result and also avoid the appearance of an autobiography, which might overshadow the original purpose. I tried it and to no one's discredit it simply didn't work. I also realized after literally months of "second-hand" effort that the only person who could write the story was I. Many times you find yourself calling upon others to create what only you can accomplish. And believe it or not, I have had fun doing this because the ideas, the happenings, the chronology, the results, good or bad, and the real "feel" of the true story seemed to flow rather effortlessly out of the end of my pen. Yes, it has been hand-written and Sally and Brenda tell me that it seemed to "flow" as they typed it all, meaning perhaps that I have accomplished my mission.

What I fondly hope is that this story in book form will find its way into younger hands, people I know or don't know, who will read it with enjoyment and that I will hopefully have inspired or motivated them into a never-visited realm of making things happen that they never dreamed possible.

Fred C. Tucker, Jr.

Let me illustrate more fully. Now over thirty years ago I sat down and devised a series of five "five year plans" which I labeled by years and subjects —all of which I hoped to accomplish. I still have those plans safely tucked away and again, believe it or not, most of them have happened and have come true! They involved family, business growth, civic involvements with target dates to meet, Real Estate Association offices and achievements, and a warm sprinkling of time for friends, the making of new friends, and a relationship to people. And a sense of God's own direction and help has ever been my constant inspiration, because I learned long ago that with Him as a Partner great and good things can and do happen.

If I were called upon to name the two most important traits, other than honesty itself, needed for a successful life and career I would name them immediately: *Enthusiasm and Imagination!* Each relies upon the other and when the two are combined any number of interesting things can happen which make others want to join in. Picture a group meeting where either or both of these traits of the leader are lacking and tell me how long the meeting will last and what the attitudes of those present will become. But fire up a meeting with pep and with some ideas for discussion and watch the lights go on around the room among all of those assembled. A leader owes both of these traits to his associates, and if he is a good listener, he will learn more from the group, thus energized, than he imparts.

Little things, developed into habits, can do wonders for growth and for morale. How many of you have a memo pad close at hand for writing off short notes to others, some of whom you've never met, either congratulating them for an achievement or consoling them in their grief? If you keep the personal memo pad nearby (not for business purposes but sent out from the heart) you will be amazed what you do for others and their well being, and your own inner satisfaction too!

And don't forget about not forgetting! Start back in time at the point of your entry into the business. Who helped you get started, who taught you, who encouraged you, and who praised your efforts - and just when was the last time you went out of your way to search them out years later, wherever they are, just to say Thank You!?! Think about it. Do it.

Epilogue

Do you believe a leader is born? Certainly not! A leader started from somewhere, just as you and I, and had that one trait of *caring* which helped him grow—caring about people, caring about excellence, and caring about results. No one could be more amazed—and amused—than my partners and I have been about the Tucker Company's growth. We didn't plan for size—we just asked good people to join in with us in our quest to be the best we could possibly be. And if we are judged favorably more for our caring or our professionalism than we are for our size then we have indeed achieved our initial goal as we worked and grew together. Thanks again—warm thanks—to you, John, Bob and Joe, for your mighty influence in helping us reach Our Dream!

Now some words about what has happened since January 1986 when we sold the Tucker Company to the younger fellows. Joe died at age 68, John has pretty well retired as an extremely sought after widower, and Bob and I have stayed pretty active with properties and challenges with which we are mutually engaged. The word "retire" doesn't appear in my dictionary. For the record I am now exactly the same age as the Tucker Company, which by some age standards in history is pretty young!

Some friends and I built two condominium projects in Naples, Florida, in the mid-70s and Ermajean serves as major domo in our condominium there as she does in our home in Indianapolis. She spends most of the winter there and I go back and forth somewhat like a yo-yo in full motion. We have been going to Naples since 1958 and have watched that delightful community grow to a population size ever-increasing but still featuring beauty, charm, and appropriate zoning and building controls always needed. We play golf frequently in both areas, Naples and Indianapolis, and have yet to distinguish ourselves in that game of fun and some frustration. I am sure at our age we will soon improve!

Ermajean and I traveled to Hong Kong and Singapore on the occasion of her seventieth birthday (she still looks fifty!) and enjoyed both, which have become our favorites. While in Singapore we spent two delightful evenings with former Indiana Governor Bob Orr, the American Ambassador to Singapore, and his peppy wife Josie. One was at a huge reception for some forty ambabassadors and their wives to Singapore given by the Swiss Embassy and the other right at the American Ambassador's residence where we were joined by the Canadian ambassador to Singapore and his wife. It was a delightful residence, but has since been sold to a wealthy Chinese for apartment developments. Singapore has a bright future on the Pacific Rim horizon. With the uncertainty of events that lie ahead for Hong Kong when China takes over that colony in 1997, Singapore will likely become the trade, economic and tourist center in that entire area. It glistens with cleanliness and is prepared now for such a dominant role in world affairs.

A few months ago I carried out a mission long on my mind by going to Ireland at the behest of an Irish real estate leader wanting me to see an estate some twenty miles below Dublin and adjacent to the Irish Sea. He has the property for sale and knew of my interest in hotels through our mutual involvements in the International Real Estate Federation to which we both belong.

Dublin city is one of the great metropolitan areas of the world. It has always held a fascination for me since our visit there a few years ago with the Elders, the Ryans, and Adele Rice and Harry Meyers. All of Ireland is populated with the most outgoing, fun-loving, generous and kind people anywhere and one is made to feel at home and a part of them instantaneously.

In a word, the property I went to see is in beautiful, rolling country in County Wicklow. It presently features a former country inn (now a private residence) with ten bedrooms, ten baths and various other rooms with high ceilings and beautiful views to the countryside in all directions. It also has a riding academy and horse barns plus an indoor arena for shows and exhibitions and the adjacent town of some 1500 people is "loaded" with typical Irish charm. My current efforts since returning home are directed towards seeing if the property could be turned into a fine eighteen-hole private golf facility which, with its proximity to Dublin, should prosper handsomely for the international and particularly the American traveler. My contacts to date include the well known golf/architect from Indianapolis, Pete Dye, and the representative of the John Nicklaus Golden Bear organization, introduced to me some years ago by my great friend,

Epilogue

Bill Armstrong, former head of the Indiana University Foundation. Bill Armstrong along with his charming wife Martha Lea, knows "everybody!"

But back to Dublin for a second. I chose to go back and forth from the city to the property by cab and on one occasion I "Americanized" the lady driver by telling her to pass and how fast to drive. I mention it only because it was the only time I've ever been berated, properly so, by an Irish woman with the polite admonition of "Sir, you watch the road and the scenery until I come to America and then you will do the driving and I'll tell you *where to go!*" Said with a smile with message imparted!

Also worthy of mention is my becoming a recent investor in a new FM radio station—WXTZ—"Ecstasy"—started up a few months ago to serve Noblesville and Indianapolis. The station is off to a fine start under the capable leadership of Mary Weiss, long known in radio circles in this area as a successful radio entrepreneur. The experience to date has been educational for me and has opened my eyes to a new subject with which I have had little familiarity. I suppose these few incidents above described are told in something of a defensive mood. That's because, although I tell all who ask if I have retired, I *certainly have not retired!* I often get the impression that those who work around me may well think that I'm the only one who doesn't think so! Ah me. Well at least the airlines carrying me back and forth to Florida would make it look like I'm pretty busy—and most of the time on those trips I usually wear coat and tie to at least look the part!

As President of Tucker Investment Company, Inc., I am responsible for the Tucker family properties, which change in size, character, and challenge as time goes on. Fred is Treasurer, Lucinda is Secretary, Ermajean is Vice President and Sally is Assistant Secretary of the Company. I also own and control the Pen-Shade shopping center and serve as Co-General Partner of the Canterbury Hotel. And so I am ever busy, intrigued by ideas and changes, and know that I am happy when I am busy.

Besides being a Senior-Active Rotarian, I became a member in 1987 of Indianapolis Junto, a lively, active, fun and loyal bunch of local men who meet each Monday noon at the Murat Shrine Club

145

for lunch, relaxation, story-telling and recounting of travels and experiences of recent date. Each member takes his turn at the informal speaker's stand telling of family, work, business and hobbies, thus no outside speakers are ever involved in the weekly programs. Ben Franklin started Junto some 250 years ago in Philadelphia and the Indianapolis group (which started up seventy years ago) meets as an outgrowth of this Ben Franklin idea of gathering weekly with friends on an informal basis. No group in my experience has included more fun and camaraderie, with just plain lack of purpose than Indianapolis Junto.

And a special word now about three other fellows whom I haven't yet mentioned with sufficient breadth, all good and loyal friends and all extremely competent in their own individual ways. Bob Johnston, "B. J." to all who know him, served as Tucker Company Operations Manager before his present title and duty of Co-Manager of the Keystone at the Crossing Residential Office along with twenty-eight-year veteran, Dave Queisser. B. J. served with devotion and commitment as team captain of both Hilton ventures during both construction and addition and ably so. He was an effective go-between in our relationship with Hilton Headquarters and I'm forever grateful for his role of leadership in those days.

Bill Birthright in effect "built" the Canterbury Hotel as liason among owners, architects, contractors and interior design people during the mid-80s. As Chief Engineer of the Tucker Company, Bill spends countless hours helping me in solving any and all construction or remodeling needs of Tucker properties.

And the dean of retail leasing in all of Indiana, Don Williams, vice president of the Tucker Company, is as loyal an ally as I've ever had. Don handles lease negotiations on our properties and demonstrates a professional competence well beyond that of most people in real estate anywhere. B. J., Bill and Don deserve everlasting thanks.

Isaiah 38:1-6 recounts the plea of Hezekiah through Isaiah the Prophet to the Lord for more time on this Earth and because Hezekiah had been such a true and faithful servant the Lord gave him "fifteen more years."

I often wonder how Hezekiah used those extra years, but I have a suspicion that he not only remained true to his commitment but that he also must have brimmed over with enthusiasm and with imagination to help others follow him in his quest for time to complete those things yet not accomplished.

Isn't it a wonderful thought that there will always be things yet to do left undone, though they will surely be taken up by those who follow! Who could have more good fortune than I in knowing that the future of the Tucker Company remains in loyal, competent, unselfish and dedicated hands.

And finally let me pay a brief tribute to the Tucker alumni who have gone out on their own and distinguished themselves so successfully since doing so. They all remain loyal and supportive to their Tucker Company roots and we are proud of each of them. Here are some of those well-known names, although not all inclusive: Hiram Rogers, Jim Schrage, Kurt Meyer, Wayne Timberman, Dave Jessee, Sr., Walt Bopp, Jock Fortune, John Laskowski, Dave Kelly, Mo Thomas, Jeff Henry, Ben Boleman, Tal Denny, Drew Augustin, Jim Singleton, Skip Higgins, Jim Close, Tom Lambert, Bob Beckmann, Bill Grossman and Jack Hogan, just to name a few.

Thank you, all of you mentioned or overlooked but not forgotten in these pages, for what each of you has meant to me, our family, our company, and our commitments. I do indeed love you all!

The Dream Came True!